Jacqueline Higuera McMahan

THE MEXICAN BREAKFAST COOKBOOK

Sweet and Spicy Morning Meals

Photographs and Book Design by
Robert McMahan

The Olive Press

ISBN: 1-881656-00-4

Printed in the United States of America

To my son, Ian
who hates mornings but loves breakfast

To my husband, Robert
who loves mornings and loves breakfast

To my son, O'Reilly
who hasn't yet made up his mind

Also by Jacqueline Higuera McMahan

California Rancho Cooking
The Salsa Book
The Red and Green Chile Cookbook
The Healthy Fiesta

TABLE OF CONTENTS

MEXICAN BREAKFAST

INTRODUCTION

It is amazing that breakfast even entered into my life because I am a night person. Morning people accept early morning in an every day sort of way. After all they see it every day. We night people don't.

I am always overcome by the beauty of morning when I am forced to get up early. The soft fuzzy light. The quietness. The stillness of the air. I say to myself at that moment of recognition, "I must do this more often." Morning should come upon one gradually and the person facing you at the breakfast table should not be too cheer-fully exhibitionistic. If my husband tiptoes in and hands me some dark as night coffee, I am then happy as a night person in the morning can be.

While living in Mexico I discovered the romance of breakfast. Before Mexico I had never known the joy of eating in a small courtyard filled with bougainvillea, shut off from the world. Even scrambled eggs tasted better here than in the house. Morning seemed far more wonderful than I had ever known it to be when tasted from this courtyard. The long remembrance of those Mexican breakfasts brought me to write this book. Also, the breadth of those breakfasts has a wide scope-in fact, all the way from huevos rancheros to menudo to chocolate cake-but that is what makes them special.

Still, it is morning, and it is Mexico. And there is a resinous smell of ocote wood, and a smell of coffee, and a faint smell of leaves, and of Morning, and even of Mexico. - D.H. Lawrence

Mexican breakfasts are almost endless in their possibilities. Mexicans place few limitations on what is proper for breakfast. Even a soup is considered the breakfast of champions. Menudo nurtures many Sunday morning crudos. For hearty breakfasting leftovers from dinner are carried in blue enameled pots by Mexican market vendors. Passing early morning stalls you can catch a whiff of delicious things simmering over braziers.

Liberate any norteamericano concepts which might keep you eating only certain things in expected places. Sybille Bedford tells in her charming book, *The Sudden View, A Mexican Journey,* of her Mexican friends in Lake Patzcuaro dining anywhere and everywhere. *"Mexican establishments, like those of Tzarist Russia, do not have an apartment especially assigned to the purpose of eating. Table and appurtenances are moved about and meals laid according to the season, the menu, the company and the mood: luncheon in the east-room today, the honeysuckle is blooming by the window. It is a genial arrangement and, provided one is neither short of space nor service, one that gives much scope to food and wine-omelet, ham and melon in the shade out-of-doors at noon; strawberries on the lawn; beef-stew in the kitchen; salmon on a nocturnal terrace; hock under the stars..."* Carry breakfast, even if it is just toast and jam, out to the garden, or under a tree, on the patio, or the coffee table in the living room. Some place where you usually don't breakfast. It will taste a little better if not different.

Probably because for half my life I hated mornings, I have had more memorable breakfasts than any other meal. Maybe the pain of an early rising made me sit up and take notice. Oh, there are corn flake mornings but people don't write books about them. They just quietly submit to them. This little volume is about the more memorable breakfasts. There is one particular Mexican breakfast that I'll always remember and always taste. The huevos rancheros in Saltillo one December morning.

CHAPTER I

BREAKFAST IN MEXICO

One of the most memorable meals I ever had in Mexico was a breakfast. It occurred during one of those times when everything could have been wrong but serendipity intervened, and everything was right. Rightfully, I should have been too tired to care. We should have been too rushed to take the time. It was a morning when every detail around me came to life and, rather than being sleepy, I noticed every flavor like a separate entity. I even remember noticing how crisp the white bolero jacket of our waiter was but the unexpected shabbiness of his black shoes.

My husband Robert and I had lived in Querétaro, Mexico for two years when we decided to make a marathon driving trip to California to visit our families for Christmas. We drove about four hundred miles and finally, very late at night, arrived at the outskirts of Saltillo without reservations. It was a pitch black night and very cold so we stopped in the entry way of the only motel we could see.

The dim 20-watt bulb over the manager's door did little to hide the seediness but, as exhausted as we were, we had no desire to look further. After a night of fitful sleeping on a lumpy mattress, we awoke early. The morning light made our surroundings worse and we departed the awful room quickly. Our appetites never fail us and we knew that after such a night, we desperately needed a good breakfast.

We made our escape to the zocálo where they were throwing buckets of water on the sidewalks and sweeping them clean. We were drawn across the square to a restaurant where we waited for a man to polish the brass on the door before he let us enter. Once inside we were stunned by the beautiful murals painted on the walls and the starched white tablecloths. Wonderful smells wafted from the kitchen. We were the only customers and they grandly gestured for us to pick our table.

The menu listed three types of hot chocolate. French. Mexican. Or Spanish. We chose French because it sounded more luxurious and we were definitely ready for luxury. It was the thickest and creamiest chocolate I ever tasted. To accompany the chocolate, the waiter brought huge hot bolillos (crusty rolls), toasted and heavily buttered. We ordered huevos rancheros, the perfect contrasts to the chocolate and the bolillos.

We could not gobble our food like the hungry travelers we were. We tasted and swooned, knowing that we were in the presence of a miracle. It was that morning , in my young twenty-four years, that I was given an example of how one taste can build upon another resulting in a crescendo of flavors...the thick chocolate, the buttered crisp bolillo, the spiciness of the sauce mating with the rich corn tortillas.

We lingered long over this breakfast, too long, even knowing that we yet had to drive through the vast emptiness of northern Mexico. Across a thousand miles we talked about THE BREAKFAST. We often wonder, after the passage of twenty-five years, if the restaurant is still there. We never would have found it if we hadn't passed a sleepless night in a flea bag motel in the middle of Mexico.

FRENCH CHOCOLATE

Think of a cup of this chocolate as a rare luxury as the taste is similar to a liquid truffle. It accompanies toast or buttered bolillos perfectly but not something as equally rich. Its luxury is meant to stand undisputed.

6 ounces of semisweet or bittersweet chocolate
   (a fine bittersweet chocolate is the best)
2 cups whole milk
2 cups half and half
2 tablespoons sugar
2 teaspoons pure vanilla

1. In a heavy- bottomed saucepan, place the chocolate, milk, cream, and sugar. Slowly stir and whisk while the mixture heats over a medium flame. Pull off the heat when little bubbles form around the edge and add the vanilla.

2. Now beat the chocolate until very foamy. In Mexico they use a molinillo which is a carved wooden stick with rings. The stick is twirled between the palms of your hand but I have found that a whisk or hand blender submerged right into the liquid does a superb job of foaming the chocolate so it is frothy. Serve the foaming French Chocolate in cups (rather than mugs).

 Serves 4 with toasted bolillos, sourdough bread, English muffins, or thick homemade bread.

THE HUEVOS RANCHEROS FROM SALTILLO

The ranchero sauce is as close an approximation of what I remember about those served in Saltillo, Mexico. In this version grated cheese is placed between the corn tortillas so you have a flat quesadilla as a base for the huevos. The chunky, spicy sauce is ladled over everything and is the key to making these huevos special.

RANCHERO SAUCE

You can make sauce the day before or just keep some in the refrigerator.

1 large can (28 ounces) ready-cut tomatoes
or plum tomatoes, drained
2 fresh tomatoes, diced
1 onion (about 1 cup), diced
3 jalapeño chiles, seeded, minced
2 cloves garlic, minced
2 tablespoons tomato paste
1/2 cup water
1 to 2 tablespoons ground red chile
1/2 teaspoon salt
1/2 teaspoon ground cumin

1. Chop the drained plum tomatoes with a chef's knife or in a food processor. Place in a saucepan with all the rest of the ingredients and simmer for fifteen minutes. Reserve sauce while you prepare other ingredients.

ASSEMBLING THE HUEVOS RANCHEROS

2 tablespoons oil
8 corn tortillas (for four people)
1 cup grated Monterey Jack or Cheddar cheese
1 to 2 tablespoons oil for frying eggs
8 eggs (2 per person)
1 cup water
Ranchero Sauce

1. Heat 1 tablespoon of oil at a time in a skillet. Place 2 heaping tablespoons of grated cheese between 2 corn tortillas. Fry each set of tortillas in the oil until the edges are crisp and the cheese melted. The tortillas should remain soft. Place tortillas on a baking sheet and keep warm in a 250 degree oven while you poach the eggs.

2. Meanwhile, the Ranchero Sauce should be heating in a saucepan

3. Fry the eggs in a nonstick skillet or poach Mexican-style. Heat one tablespoon of oil in a 12 to 14-inch nonstick skillet (that has a lid or improvise one). When the skillet is medium hot, crack in four eggs. Cover with 1/2 cup of the water. Place on the lid and allow the eggs to steam-poach over medium heat for two to four minutes depending upon how firm you want them. After four minutes they will be fairly firm. Use a spatula to separate the eggs, cutting them into squares. Place two eggs each on two of the tortilla stacks. Drain off any remaining water. Add a bit more oil to the skillet, place back on heat, and crack in four more eggs. Add 1/2 cup more water for poaching and place on lid. Cook as before.

When all the tortilla stacks have their required eggs, transfer to warm plates and spoon about 1/2 cup hot Ranchero Sauce over the eggs. Serve with refried beans, warm bolillos, and hot chocolate or cafe con leche.

Serves 4.

A SINGLE GIRL'S MEXICAN BREAKFAST
BAKED BANANAS IN SKINS

When I first moved to San Miguel de Allende, Mexico I attended the Instituto Allende and shared with three other girls a huge 300 - year old colonial house known as Hospicio 8. For the princely sum of $40 per person, the house provided a courtyard, a roof garden, four bed-rooms, a huge kitchen, sala, and resident ghosts. Between classes and time spent in small cafes of the village, no one cooked or had much money to spend on food.

That is when Beryl, with whom I shared a common love of anything to eat, discovered the joys of baked bananas. Beryl cracked several of Hospicio 8's good blue-glazed terra cotta dishes by baking bananas on them. Pie plates work the best.

Place bananas, intact in their skins, in a preheated 350 degree oven and bake for 15 minutes. The skins will blacken and the bananas will become a natural pudding. Use a small knife to slit the length of each baked banana from end to end. Sprinkle liberally with sugar and cin-namon. If we were rich, we had some crema doble over the hot, creamy banana. With this repast you need only a cup of cafe con leche and then you can count yourself lucky that day. This simple meal sustained us for many Mexican mornings.

SCRAMBLED SUNDAY MORNING EGGS WITH TORTILLA STRIPS

Whether it is a Salvadoran, Mexican, or Nicaraguan home, Sunday is patriarchal. Papa calls the shots.

It is Papa's honored role to visit the panadería to buy a mountain of sweet rolls or pan dulce. The panadería is probably in the part of town where he might run into a few cronies and have to stop for a cafecito and cigar. Back at home everyone is trying to get the Sunday breakfast together. It might be huevos rancheros, Spanish rice, refried beans, salpicón, or spicy scrambled eggs like those below. Most importantly Mama chops salsa with a mountain of chiles. If the salsa isn't hot enough, she will certainly hear about it from Papa's end of the table.

The excitement of what he will bring home continues to mount throughout the morning. Sometimes he includes a small gift for Mama like perfume or candies for the children. When he finally comes through the door, strutting with his packages and a big carton of greasy menudo, everyone dives for the bags of pan dulce to fight over the pink ones. The pink ones taste the best. My Nicaraguan friend, Janet, says that her father always brought champagne. Each child got a shot glass of bubbly to toast Sunday breakfast and the dog, who really preferred beer, drank his toast out of Papa's cigar ashtray.

The main feature of any Mexican-cum-Grande Sunday morning breakfast is lots of different foods. Try to find a market with pan dulce and bolillos or use crusty French rolls. Make beans or rice to accompany your main dish. You can precook the peppers and chile for the scrambled eggs below making them much easier to prepare than huevos rancheros when you are dealing with a crowd. In the recipe below, the delicious last touch are the strips of crisp corn tortillas which soften after adding to the scrambled eggs. If you are in a hurry, you may crumble 12 tortilla chips into the eggs instead of the tortillas. Use a good brand or the new oil-free Guiltless Gourmet chips.

3 tablespoons canola oil
3 stale corn tortillas, cut into narrow strips
1 tablespoon olive oil
1 red bell pepper, cored and diced
2 jalapeño chiles, seeded, minced
5 green onions, minced
3 plum tomatoes, minced
3 ounces cream cheese (keeps scrambled eggs moist)
12 large eggs, beaten

1. In one batch at a time, fry the tortilla strips until they are crisp but not too brown. Drain on paper towels. Set aside.

2. In the tablespoon of olive oil, sauté the red pepper, jalapeños, green onions, and plum tomatoes for five minutes. Into this mixture, blend the cream cheese, about a tablespoon at a time. Remove from heat until you are ready to add the eggs.

3. When you are ready to scramble in the eggs, put the pan with the pepper-cream cheese mixture over medium heat and pour in the beaten eggs. Stir continually. Just before they are completely set, stir in the crisp tortilla strips or chips. Keep stirring so that they are evenly distributed and the eggs are done but still creamy. Serve immediately. These eggs are delicious with a little hot salsa on the side, along with fruit and the pan dulce that Papa brought home.

Serves 6.

BANANA FRITTERS

When Beryl and I weren't baking bananas we were making these fritters. They are delicious for brunch or to accompany any Mexican breakfast (lunch or dinner). The batter is light and the Banana Fritters taste good hours later but they are at their perfection when still warm.

6 firm bananas, peeled and halved
1 cup all-purpose, unbleached flour
2 teaspoons baking powder
1/2 teaspoon salt
1/4 cup sugar
1/2 cup milk
1 egg
1 teaspoon vanilla
1 tablespoon vegetable oil
2 cups canola oil for frying
2 tablespoons sugar plus
  1 teaspoon cinnamon for sprinkling

1. Sift flour, baking powder, salt, and sugar together. Beat milk, egg, vanilla, and vegetable oil together. Add to the dry ingredients stirring just until blended. Add a couple of teaspoons more milk if the batter seems too stiff.

2. While you are doing this the oil can be heating for the frying process. A deep 3-quart saucepan or an electric skillet can be used. Cover a large platter or baking sheet with several thicknesses of paper towels.

3. Heat oil to 360 degrees or test by dropping a teaspoon of batter into the oil. If it sizzles and turns golden the oil is ready. Place 2 banana quarters at a time in the batter and then gently lower into the hot oil. As the fritters cook, use a spatula to turn them over, making sure they do not stick to the bottom of the pan. Cook the fritters until they are golden on both sides. Then place on paper towels and blot to remove oil.

4. Sprinkle the warm Banana Fritters with cinnamon sugar. When they are warm the insides are like banana pudding. The outsides remain crisp even when they are slightly cool. Makes 24 fritters. Serves 8 or less if you are serving children.

IF YOU DO NOT HAVE SOMEONE BRINGING PAN DULCE, THE BANANA FRITTERS MAKE A WONDERFUL SUBSTITUTE.

HUEVOS MOTULEÑOS

The first time I ate Huevos Motuleños, the Huevos Rancheros of Yucatan, I was amused by the curiosity of peas and ham over eggs served in a jungle. I wondered who created such a recipe. My favorite thing about them is that they are traditionally accompanied by sautéed bananas (yes, bananas again) and black beans. Serve them to your friends who long for the exotic.

The salsa served over the huevos is not picante. Most tables in Yucatan have a bowl of xnipec sand if you want anything hot, it will give you fire in one spoonful. Below is a recipe for mild Yucatan salsa where one chile is just floated through the salsa for flavor.

YUCATAN SALSA FOR HUEVOS

1 tablespoon olive oil
4 tomatoes, seared over flame or broiled
1/4 cup chopped onion
1 clove minced garlic
1 teaspoon vinegar
1 bay leaf
1 whole habanero or serrano chile (leave intact)

1. Remove as much of the blackened skin as possible from tomatoes and then chop with a knife or in chop coarsely in a food processor.

2. Heat olive oil in skillet and sauté onions until softened-for a couple of minutes and then add rest of ingredients: the chopped tomatoes, the garlic, vinegar, bay leaf,

and whole chile. The chile is added for flavor rather than heat. Simmer for ten minutes. Set aside. You can easily make this salsa the day before you need it. Warm just before serving.

ASSEMBLING HUEVOS

Yucatan Salsa, from above recipe
1 to 2 tablespoons canola oil for frying tortillas
8 corn tortillas
1 tablespoon canola oil and 1 tablespoon butter
  for frying bananas
2 firm bananas or 1 plantain (plátano macho)
1 cup diced ham
2 cups Pureed Black Beans (recipe below)
1/2 cup cooked frozen peas
2 tablespoons canola oil for frying eggs
8 eggs, or 2 eggs person
1/3 cup finely grated Parmesan cheese or queso fresco

1. Fry all the corn tortillas in oil, adding more oil if necessary. You want them to be crisp around the edges but to remain pliable. Keep warm in oven.

2. After you have finished the tortillas, wipe out the skillet with paper towels and add a tablespoon of fresh oil and a tablespoon of butter. Peel the bananas, split lengthwise and quarter. Sauté the banana pieces until golden. If you are using plantains, you will have to sauté them ten minutes longer. Keep warm in oven.

3. In the same skillet, sauté the diced ham just until browned on the edges. Remove and set aside. Use the same skillet to warm the black beans. If you plan your

cooking steps, you can really get mileage out of one skillet and not use a lot of pans. If you prepared the recipe for the black beans using the recipe below you will just need to heat up two cups. Leave beans whole or puree in food processor. In Yucatan they push them through a sieve. Or use canned black beans if you are pressed for time.

4. Fry the eggs according to your guests' personal taste. This is the last step before assembling the Huevos Motuleños.

5. Place two warm corn tortillas slightly overlapping on each plate. Spread 1/2 cup black beans over tortillas. Next place the fried eggs on top of beans. Spoon on about 1/2 cup warm salsa. Over the salsa, sprinkle the ham and peas. Over this sprinkle a couple of teaspoons of grated Parmesan. Lay the fried bananas as garnish along the sides of the plates.

Serves 4 hungry breakfast eaters who won't need to eat the rest of the day.

SPICY BLACK BEANS

Black beans are always served as an accompaniment to foods in southern Mexican.

1 pound black beans
10 cups water for soaking
8 cups fresh water for cooking
1 tablespoon olive oil
1 red onion, chopped
4 cloves garlic, minced

1 serrano chile, minced
1 teaspoon ground cumin
4 bay leaves
2 tablespoons cider vinegar
2 teaspoons salt

1. Under running water rinse beans in sieve, removing any stones or grit. Place in large pot, cover with water. Bring to a boil and simmer for three minutes. Turn off heat and allow beans to steep for at least one to three hours. Discard soaking water.

2. Add fresh water to beans and again bring to a simmer and cook until tender. Presoaked beans will cook in about one and a half to two hours. If you cook in a pressure cooker, they will be done in one hour.

3. Meanwhile, in olive oil sauté the onion until softened. Add the minced garlic, chile, spices, and bay leaves. When beans are tender to the bite, drain off some of the cooking water (reserve for later use) and add the onion mixture. Stir in vinegar and salt. Simmer the spiced beans for 20 to 30 minutes longer.

If you want to serve sieved beans Yucatan-style, push 1 and 1/2 cups beans through sieve or puree in a food processor, adding 1/3 cup bean cooking liquid. Heat 1 tablespoon oil in skillet, add beans and liquid. Heat until bubbly. Sprinkle with crumbled queso fresco or Parmesan.

Serves 8 as a side dish

BAY LEAVES, WHEN ADDED TO BEANS, GIVE A
SUBTLE SWEETNESS.

MEXICO CITY CHILAQUILES

Tortillas, the staff of life in Mexico, are never wasted. Stale tortillas find their way into the fondest of breakfast meals-Chilaquiles. Chilaquiles are just crisp strips of fried tortillas briefly simmered in salsa. You can also add chicken, chorizo, ham, or sour cream. The worst thing you can do is cook the Chilaquiles too long and end up with a dried up gringo casserole.

1/3 cup canola oil
8 stale, day-old corn tortillas, cut into eighths
1/2 cup chopped onion
2 Anaheim chiles, charred, skinned, cut into strips
1 and 1/2 cups green salsa, homemade (see recipe be-low)
   or store-bought
1/2 cup chicken broth
1 sprig fresh epazote or
   1 teaspoon dried epazote (optional but traditional)
1 tablespoon cilantro, minced
1 cup Monterey Jack cheese, grated
1/3 cup sour cream,
   thinned with 1 tablespoon milk

1. Heat oil in a heavy, 12-inch skillet and fry about one-third of the tortilla pieces at a time. Turn frequently until they are golden and crisp. Drain on paper towels and blot off any excess oil.

2. When you are finished frying the tortilla wedges, drain off any remaining oil. In just the remaining glaze of oil in the pan, sauté the chopped onion until softened but not brown. Next stir in the green chiles. If you have the time to char a couple of chiles, peel, and chop them. The flavors will be far superior to canned chiles. Add the green sauce, chicken broth, epazote, and cilantro. Bring to a gentle simmer and then add the crisp tortilla wedges. Simmer for just five minutes. Sprinkle on the grated cheese. Serve on each plate garnished with avocado slices and more cilantro. Drizzle the thinned sour cream over the top of each serving.

Serves 4.

WHEN THE CRISP TORTILLA WEDGES ARE IMMERSED IN THE SIMMERING SALSA, THEY SOFTEN IN A MATTER OF MINUTES MAKING CHILAQUILES A VERY FAST BREAKFAST DISH. DO NOT OVERCOOK! MANY CAFES MAKE THEM IN INDIVIDUAL SKILLETS FOR EASIER SERVING.

FAST SALSA VERDE (GREEN SALSA)

This is one of the best green salsas that I know. Personally, I do not like the taste of tomatillos after they have cooked for fifteen to twenty minutes which is what many recipes advise. The fresh, citrony taste of tomatillos is preserved when they are barely cooked and so a brief cooking in the microwave oven is one of the best methods to use.

l and 1/2 pounds fresh tomatillos
4 jalapeño chiles or serrano chiles, stems removed
3 cloves garlic
1/2 cup cilantro
1 teaspoon vinegar
1/2 teaspoon salt
1/2 teaspoon sugar

1. Place tomatillos in a sink of warm water to soak for a few minutes to soften the dry husks. Peel off husks. Place tomatillos on a flat dinner plate. Microwave on high power for 225 seconds (for a 600 watt oven). Steam for two minutes if you do not have a microwave oven.

2. Place cooked tomatillos in a food processor with all the rest of the ingredients and coarsely puree. Cut chiles into pieces before adding to food processor. If you are using jalapeños, discard just the cores. Keep the seeds to add to the salsa. In Mexico, the entire serrano chile is used. They are too small to bother with removing seeds. Store salsa in a glass jar. Makes about one quart and will keep well for several days. You can freeze it but it will separate when thawed. Simmer in a saucepan for two minutes and it will thicken again.

HUEVOS EN SALSA VERDE

One of the best breakfast uses for the green sauce above is to simmer scrambled eggs in the salsa. Simple and heavenly and very typically Mexican.

1 and 1/2 cups of Fast Salsa Verde
  or your own green sauce
1/2 cup water
Small sprig of epazote (optional but traditional)
1 tablespoon canola oil or olive oil
8 eggs, beaten

1. After you have made the Salsa Verde, add 1/2 cup water and epazote and simmer in a ten-inch skillet for five minutes.

2.   Heat the oil in a nonstick skillet, add the beaten eggs, and cook just to the soft stage. When they are just barely done and still moist around the edges, immediately place them into the skillet with the heated Salsa Verde. Cook for about another minute or just long enough for the salsa to penetrate the eggs.   Stir frequently. Serves 4 with beans and tortillas.

HUEVOS EN SALSA VERDE ARE DELICIOUS STUFFED INTO A BREAKFAST BURRITO WITH BEANS OR POTATOES.

VERACRUZ CHILAQUILES

This is a savory red version of chilaquiles which is a bit more filling because you can add chicken or sautéed chorizo sausage. Ideally, you can make this when you have leftover, cooked chicken or sausage.

1/3 cup canola oil
8 tortillas, cut into eighths
1 pound tomatoes, broiled (about 2 large tomatoes)
2 cloves garlic, minced
3/4 cup diced red onion
1 ancho chile, toasted
1 sprig of fresh epazote (optional)
1/2 teaspoon salt
1 and 1/2 cups chicken broth
1/2 chicken breast, poached in above broth
*   or 1/4 pound sautéed chorizo*
3/4 cup Mexican crema doble
*   or 1/2 cup sour cream and 2 tablespoons*
*   half and half*
1 cup grated medium sharp Cheddar cheese

1. Fry the tortilla wedges, a few at a time, in the oil until they are crisp and golden. Drain on paper towels and blot. Set aside. You can do this the night before if needed. It is also at this point that it is a good time to poach the chicken breast if you haven't done so. Simmer the 1/2 breast for 20 minutes in the 1 and 1/2 cups broth. Reserve chicken broth when finished poaching.

2. Toast the dried ancho chile in a skillet for a couple of minutes. Then cover chile with boiling water and allow it to steep for twenty minutes.

3. Meanwhile, broil the tomatoes for about ten minutes or until they are slightly charred. When you can handle them, remove skins.

4. Place soaked chile in blender along with the tomatoes. Puree.

5. Remove most of the oil from skillet used to fry tortilla wedges and sauté the onion until softened. Add minced garlic. Holding a wire strainer over the skillet, pour the tomato-ancho mixture into the strainer and work it through with the back of a large spoon to remove tomato and chile skins from sauce. Add epazote, salt, and 1/2 cup of the reserved chicken broth. Simmer sauce for about twenty minutes. If sauce seems too thick add 1/4 cup more chicken broth.

6. Cut poached chicken into thin strips or sauté 1/4 pound chorizo for 10 minutes.

7. Add the crisp tortilla wedges to the simmering tomato-chile sauce. Stir them around so they begin to soften. This just takes 2 to 3 minutes. Add the chicken or sautéed chorizo. Now pour everything into an oven proof baking dish. Drizzle crema doble or sour cream mixture over the top and sprinkle with grated cheese. Place 8 inches under a hot broiler for 3 to 5 minutes or until cheese is bubbling. Do not brown. Serve immediately. Serves 4 to 6 and recipe easily doubles.

GUATEMALAN CHILAQUILES

Even though these are called chilaquiles, they bear little resemblance to Mexican chilaquiles. The tortillas used should be fresh so they don't crack when folded. These are a unique way to cook chiles tortillas rellenos.

1/2 cup chopped onion
2 cups grated Jack and Italian Fontina cheese (1 cup of each)
5 fresh green chiles (Anaheim or New Mexican), charred
10 corn tortillas
3 eggs, separated
1/4 teaspoon salt
1 tablespoon flour
1/4 cup canola oil
Chirmol Sauce or regular tomato salsa, warmed

1. Mix the onion and cheese together. Remove the blackened skins from the green chiles. Remove stems and seeds. Cut into wide strips.

2. You may have to warm each tortilla on a griddle or comal just for a few seconds. They fold much easier when warm and pliable. On bottom half of each corn tortilla, place two tablespoons cheese-onion mixture and 2 strips of green chile.   Fold over top half of tortilla.

3. Heat the oil in a skillet over medium heat. Beat egg whites to firm peaks using a whisk or mixer. Beat salt and flour into yolks and then fold into the whites. One at a time, dip folded tortilla into the egg batter and gently

slide into the skillet. Fry just until golden. Place in a baking dish (9 x 13 inches) or cookie sheet. Continue on with the dipping and frying of all the folded tortillas. You can do everything up to this step and then hold the chilaquiles as they will repuff in the hot oven.

4. Just before serving time, place chilaquiles in a preheated 375 degree oven and bake for 10 minutes. The chilaquiles will repuff and cheese will melt. Serve with Chirmol Sauce drizzled over each serving.

CHIRMOL SAUCE

3 tomatoes, broiled
1/4 cup chopped onion
1 clove garlic, minced
1 whole dried red pepper, arból or japonés
1/2 teaspoon salt
1/4 teaspoon sugar
1 teaspoon vinegar

1. Broil the tomatoes until skins are slightly charred. When you can handle them remove skins. Place tomatoes in a food processor with onion and garlic. Chop to a fairly smooth sauce.

2. Simmer in a saucepan for 15 minutes, adding the whole pepper (broken in half), salt, sugar, and vinegar.

Makes 1 and 1/2 cups.

VERACRUZ BREAKFAST TACOS

In Veracruz, on the Gulf coast of southern Mexico, the vendors serve some of the best soft tacos with unusual fillings. It was always a difficult choice to decide on pan-fried red snapper or a soft taco filled with scrambled eggs and nopalitos (cactus) in red chile sauce.

1/2 pound fresh nopales (cactus)
1 can (1 pound, 12 ounces) red chile sauce (Las Palmas)
2 cloves minced garlic
1/2 cup chopped onion
2 teaspoons oregano
1 teaspoon crushed cumin seed
1/4 cup minced cilantro
1 tablespoon oil for cooking scrambled eggs
8 beaten eggs
8 corn tortillas

1. First prepare cactus. Hold the cactus with tongs or lay on paper towels while you use a small, sharp paring knife to slice off node of each spine. If you are lucky enough to find very young nopales, the spines will be barely existent. There will be little green sprouts where the spines have not yet grown out. Trim around edge of cactus paddle where nodes are closer together. Trim off blunt end where cactus paddle was cut from plant. Do not peel outer skin from the nopal. Peeling is unnecessary and causes the nopal to release juices.

2. Drop the cactus into 4 quarts of simmering water. Cook for 2 minutes and then place in colander. Rinse with cold water. Dice the nopalitos. Rinse out pot. You can substitute nopalitos from a jar but be sure and rinse well.

3. Into pot, place the chile sauce, garlic, onion, oregano, cumin, and cilantro. Simmer for 15 minutes and then add the diced cactus. Simmer for another 15 minutes. Set aside while you prepare the scrambled eggs and heat the tortillas.

4. Heat the oil in a nonstick skillet. Scramble the eggs. Warm the corn tortillas on a comal or wrap in foil and heat in a 350 degree F. oven for about 10 minutes.

5. Fill each warm, soft tortilla with a couple of tablespoons of scrambled egg drizzled with a tablespoon of nopalitos in red chile. This recipe makes 2 tacos per person for 4 people and you will have some nopalitos left for tomorrow morning.

OAXACAN COLORADITO SAUCE OVER EGGS

One of the great joys of being in Oaxaca is eating some form of mole all day long. Oaxaca is famous for having seven moles, just one of them being coloradito. It is not as complex nor as sweet as the dark mole with chocolate but is the perfect mole to spoon over fried or poached eggs. Accompany with black beans and tortillas to sop up more sauce. Coloradito sauce also makes great enchiladas just filled with chicken and sprinkled with crumbled queso fresco or goat cheese.

The principal chile used here is the dried ancho which has a rich, sweet flavor.

8 ancho chiles
4 guajillo chiles
2 large tomatoes
1/2 onion
4 cloves garlic
1/4 cup sesame seeds, toasted
1/4 cup almonds, toasted
1 tablespoon raisins
1 tablespoon oil
1 plantain or plátano macho
  or substitute 1/4 of a banana
1 pan dulce or slice of French bread
2 teaspoons dried oregano
3 cloves, crushed
1/2 teaspoon freshly ground pepper
1/2 teaspoon salt
2 teaspoons sugar
1 2-inch piece cinnamon
1 to 2 cups chicken broth for thinning sauce

1. Toast all the chiles in a dry pan or on a griddle. The chiles should soften and barely change color so as not to burn. This takes about three minutes. Cover chiles with boiling water and steep for 1 hour with lid over bowl.

2. In a deep pan, place the tomatoes, onion half, and garlic. Broil about 8 inches from flame until tomatoes are a bit charred and skins are loosened.

3. While the tomatoes are broiling, toast the sesame seeds and almonds in the oven or toaster oven for about 7 minutes at 350 degrees. Set aside.

4. Skin the plantain and cut in long diagonal slices. Fry in the tablespoon of oil for ten minutes until golden. If you do not have a plantain, do not use a whole banana as a substitute as the banana has a much fruitier and sweeter flavor than the plátano macho. In place of plantain, use 1/4 of banana but you do not have to cook it.

5. Remove stems from the soaked chiles and most of their seeds. Place in blender jar to puree with the tomatoes, onions, and garlic. Add 1 cup of the chile soaking liquid. If soaking liquid tastes bitter just use water.

6. Pour the chile-tomato mixture into a wire strainer over a large bowl and push through with a spoon. Place 1 cup of the strained sauce back into the blender jar. Add the sesame seeds, almonds, raisins, crushed cloves, oregano, sautéed plantain, and pan dulce. Blend until the seeds and nuts are finely pureed with the sauce. Place this mixture and the rest of the tomato-chile mixture to simmer in a deep 3-quart saucepan. Simmer for

20 minutes. Add salt and sugar. Stir frequently as mole tends to splatter right out of the pan if you don't watch and stir frequently. You will probably have to add broth a little at a time. This is a sauce that is best made the day before you plan on using it. It keeps well for a week in the refrigerator and freezes well.

Makes about 1 quart.

TO SERVE COLORADITO SAUCE OVER EGGS

Fry the number of eggs per person that you wish to serve. Cover eggs with warm Coloradito Sauce, crumbled queso fresco, and serve a side of black beans. A couple of rings of pickled red onion make a pretty garnish. You can pickle red onion in a flash by just mixing 1/2 cup cider vinegar with 1 cup water. Slice a red onion into this liquid and simmer for 1 minute. You can also cook on high in a microwave for 1 minute. Use these onion rings as a garnish or on sandwiches.

QUESILLO EN SALSA

One of the most famous cheeses of Oaxaca is the quesillo, sold in the marketplace in little balls (bolas) similar in flavor to our mozzarella cheese but much richer. The closest we can come to the native cheese is to use the fresh mozzarella sold in Italian markets. If all else fails use pieces of the standard mozzarella available in grocery stores.

The little bolas of cheese are covered in warm, light tomato sauce making an excellent accompaniment to spicy brunch dishes. I first tasted Quesillo En Salsa during a Sunday brunch held at our hotel in Oaxaca and I ate more of it than anything else. It makes a good side to any of the Mexican egg dishes.

2 ancho chiles
2 pounds tomatoes, broiled
1 jalapeño chile, seeded, minced
1 onion, chopped
1 clove garlic, minced
1 tablespoon oil
1 tablespoon cider vinegar
1 teaspoon salt
1/2 teaspoon cayenne pepper
1/2 teaspoon sugar
1 branch fresh epazote or 1 teaspoon dried epazote
1 pound bolas de quesillo or fresh mozzarella balls

1. Rinse the dried ancho chiles under cold water. Break off stems and remove seeds. Cover with boiling water. Allow the chiles to steep for at least 30 minutes.

2. Meanwhile, take care of the tomatoes. Place them under a broiler until they are charred and skins are loosened. This may take about 6 to 8 minutes. When you can handle them, remove the skins.

3. Place the soaked ancho chiles in a food processor with the tomatoes, onion, and garlic. Chop to a coarse puree. Push through a strainer.

4. Heat oil in a large skillet and add the tomato-chile puree along with the vinegar, salt, cayenne, sugar, and epazote. Simmer for 20 minutes. Remove sauce from heat and add the bolas or pieces of cheese. The cheese will warm slightly and soften but it should not melt. Serve the quesillo slightly warm to accompany the rest of the breakfast. Accompany with corn tortillas to sop up the sauce.

EVERYWHERE IN THE MARKETPLACES OF OAXACA IN THE SUMMER MONTHS YOU FIND LARGE BUNDLES OF FRESH EPAZOTE. OAXACAN COOKS PUT 6-INCH SPRIGS OR RAMAS OF THIS FRESH HERB IN JUST ABOUT EVERY SAUCE THAT THEY COOK AND THEY ALWAYS PUT EPAZOTE IN BLACK BEANS.

BAJA CORN TORTILLAS

I have played around with corn tortillas for years because they are one of the most common things I have heard people complain about making. Using the fresh masa and learning to form it into tortillas is difficult the first time. Patting tortillas by hand out of corn masa, hand-ground on a metate is part of Mexico's national heritage which is rapidly disappearing. There are tortillerías or tortilla factories in practically every little town in Mexico. But once you have tasted freshly made corn tortillas you are hooked. This is not something you do all the time. Maybe just for special occasion Mexican dining. But it is worth it.

I have found that by adding a little regular all-purpose flour and a touch of oil, the dough adheres better. Recently, on a trip to Cabo San Lucas we ate twice in the Mi Casa restaurant and had some of the best food we have ever eaten in Mexico. Every evening a special tortilla cook is kept busy patting out tortillas. When I commented on how delicate and sweet they were, the owner told me that they mixed in regular flour along with the masa. This makes the dough easier to handle.

2 cups masa harina
1/4 cup all-purpose flour
1 cup warm water plus 2 to 4 tablespoons more water
3 teaspoons canola oil

1. Masa harina, the dehydrated version of freshly ground masa, is a flavorful corn flour that makes a good substitute. Dump the masa harina, the flour, 1 cup plus 2 tablespoons water, and the oil into the bowl of a food

processor. Whirl just until combined.   If the dough doesn't adhere together and form a nice soft mass, it needs the extra tablespoons of water. Whirl again. The dough should stick together but not be gummy or wet. I promise you that ultimately you will have a "feel" for the dough. Wrap dough up in plastic wrap or a plastic bag. Let it sit for 15 minutes at room temperature.

2. Heat the comal or griddle for cooking the tortillas.

3. Cut out two squares of plastic, slightly larger than your tortilla press. Place one square of plastic on the bottom half of the press. In the middle of square place a ball of dough (about size of a unshelled walnut). Place the next square of plastic on top of dough. Lower the upper portion of press. Press down on handle to mold the tortilla.

4.   Holding the tortilla and bottom plastic on the fingers of one hand, peel off the top plastic. I have found the peeling from the sides works the best. Place the tortilla on medium hot griddle, comal, or frying pan. Cook the tortilla until little freckles start to form and then turn. Cook for about a minute.   Place warm tortilla in foil so it doesn't dry out. Continue making rest of tortillas. Serve within the hour or keep wrapped in foil and reheat before serving.   Freshly made corn tortillas do not keep quite as well as flour tortillas because they do not have the fat content.

Makes 12 corn tortillas.

Quesadilla dough is formed like a corn tortilla using the press; dough is filled; turnover is formed and then fried.

QUESADILLA TURNOVERS

Most of us think of a quesadilla as a flour tortilla folded over some cheese and lightly fried until golden. The real Mexican quesadilla is a little turnover made from corn tortilla dough. But I have a discovered a much more workable and delicious substitute by adapting a recipe of Elizabeth Lambert Ortiz, creating a more flavorful dough, easier to work with, and one which results in a golden, crusty turnover similar in crunch to a pupusa.

These are not difficult to put together and are great for breakfast or a snack.

2 cups masa harina (dehydrated masa, see index)
1/4 cup all-purpose flour
1/2 teaspoon salt
1/2 teaspoon baking powder
2 tablespoons canola oil
1 egg
1/2 cup low-fat milk
1/4 cup warm water
Choice of fillings: sautéed chorizo, strips of chile and cheese and squash blossoms or diced, cooked potatoes and cheese or just grated cheese
1/2 cup canola oil

1. Mix masa harina, flour, salt, and baking powder.

2. Drizzle in oil. Beat egg with milk and add to the dough, mixing with your fingers or a large spoon. Add the warm water. The dough should be soft and pliable but not sticky.

3. Form a 1 and 1/2-inch ball of dough and press in a tortilla press fitted with 2 squares of plastic. Form just as you do the corn tortillas. See recipe above for Baja Tortillas.

4. Place the circle of dough on a board and on bottom half of circle, spoon in 3 teaspoons of filling. Fold over top half and press across top evenly with palm of hand and then press edges together. This recipe makes about 10 quesadilla turnovers.

5. Heat the canola oil in a deep skillet and fry 3 quesadillas at a time. Cook until golden brown on one side and then turn and cook on the other side. Drain on paper towels when you remove each quesadilla from pan and immediately blot. If you do this they will absorb very little oil.

QUESADILLA FILLINGS

1/2 cup cooked, diced potatoes
1/2 cup cooked chorizo
> *or*
2 green chiles (Anaheim, New Mexican, or poblano)
  char chiles over flame, peel, and seed
3/4 cup grated Monterey Jack cheese or Chihuahu a
  cheese
> *or*
1 tablespoon olive oil
4 or 5 minced squash blossoms (flor de calabaza)
1 clove minced garlic
2 tablespoons minced onion
1 tablespoon minced fresh epazote (optional)
1 green chile (Anaheim, New Mexican or poblano)
  charred over flame, peeled, and seeded

1/2 teaspoon salt
3/4 cup grated Monterey Jack cheese

1. Squash blossoms are one of the most dearly loved and traditional fillings for quesadillas along with huitlacoche, the corn fungus considered to be the Mexican equivalent of truffles.   Sauté the minced flores in the olive oil along with the garlic, onion, epazote, chile, and salt for 5 minutes. Set aside and then mix with the cheese for the quesadilla filling.

2. Fill and fry quesadillas as instructed above.

MACHACA CON HUEVOS

This very típico breakfast is found not only in Mexico but wherever you find the greater Mexican population outside of Mexico-it's common in parts of San Diego, East L.A., Oxnard, and one of our favorite cafes in Santa Fe, New Mexico. Probably anywhere in the world where there is a old-style Mexican cook, there is machaca. Traditionally, it's made with dried beef just as it was in the old days. But now many cooks just use a tender pot roast or brisket that has been simmered until it falls apart and then the meat is shredded so that it is stringy like jerky. The smartest thing to do is cook pot roast for dinner and then reserve part of it for machaca.

1 3-pound chuck roast or beef brisket
1 tablespoon oil
2 tablespoons tomato paste
1 tablespoon ground red chile
2 cloves garlic, minced through press
3 bay leaves
1/2 cup water

1. Dry meat with paper towels and brown on both sides in oil heated in Dutch oven or other heavy casserole with lid. When meat is well-browned, rub with tomato paste, ground chile, and garlic. Place bay leaves on top of meat, add water, and cover.

2. Place in preheated 350 degree oven for about 2 and 1/2 hours or until meat is fork tender. Check after 1 and 1/2 to make sure there is still water in bottom of pot. You may have to add another one-half cup water.

3. Cut off about a half pound of the cooked roast. To prepare the machaca, cut the meat into 3-inch chunks. Using two forks, pull the meat apart into shreds. It is important to shred the meat while it is still warm. If you wait, the protein solidifies. You should have about 2 cups shredded meat. Reserve for the machaca.

TO COMPLETE MACHACA

6 10-inch flour tortillas
1 tablespoon oil
1/2 cup chopped onion
1 tomato or 2 plum tomatoes, diced
1 clove minced garlic
2 serrano chiles, minced (do not remove seeds)
2 Anaheim or New Mexican green chiles, chopped
4 eggs, beaten
1/2 teaspoon salt

1. Wrap tortillas in foil and warm in a 350 degree oven for ten minutes so that they are pliable. At the same time, place the shredded beef in a pan and heat, uncovered, in the oven for ten minutes.

2. Heat the tablespoon of oil in a large skillet and sauté the onion until softened. Stir in the tomato, garlic, and chiles and cook for 3 minutes. Next stir in the 2 cups shredded beef.

3. Add the beaten eggs and salt; cook for a minute. The eggs just bind everything together and are barely there. This should not look like scrambled eggs!

4. Remove the tortillas from oven and place about one-half cup Machaca Con Huevos down the center of each one. Fold over the top and bottom of tortilla and roll up into a neatly packaged burrito. Serve with salsa.

Serves 6.

FRIJOLES CHARROS

These have become our favorite bean concoctions because they have so much more flavor than just beans. They should be served in something like little clay pots or pottery dishes along with their flavorful bean juices. They are a perfect accompaniment to any of the Mexican breakfast dishes.

1 pound pinto beans
7 cups water
3 cloves garlic, minced
1/2 onion
1 teaspoon salt, added last 30 minutes

---

3 strips bacon, diced
1 tablespoon olive oil
1 onion, diced
2 tomatoes, diced
1 clove garlic, minced
3 to 4 serrano chiles, minced
1/4 cup cilantro, minced

1. Rinse the beans in a sieve and pick out any stones. Place in a large pot and cover with cold water. Bring to a boil and simmer for three minutes. Remove beans from heat and steep from 1 to 3 hours. Pour off the

41

soaking water and add 7 cups of fresh water, the garlic, and onion. Simmer until the beans are tender and then add salt.

2. Fry bacon until almost crisp. Remove bacon to paper towel and discard the bacon fat from the pan.

3. Heat the olive oil in the same pan that you used for the bacon and sauté the diced tomatoes, onion, garlic, and serrano chiles just for a minute. Stir these vegetables into the pot of beans. Crumble the bacon and add to the beans along with cilantro. Simmer for five more minutes just to blend flavors. The Frijoles Charros are spooned into bowls with some of their liquid.

Serves 8.

THE BEST MOLLETES

Molletes, one of the most common breakfast foods in Mexico, are one of its best kept secrets for I have never eaten them in the United States except in my own kitchen. They couldn't be simpler and, along with quesadillas, qualify as one of Mexico's fast foods. Mashed beans are spread on a split bolillo half, sprinkled with a grated white cheese like Chihuahua or Jack and then placed under a broiler until the bolillo is crisp and the cheese bubbling.

My favorite mollete story is from our days in Querétaro, Mexico. We had taken some student friends to our favorite restaurant where on Sundays we liked to sit upstairs at a table overlooking a balcony and the street below.

We ordered pecan waffles and fresh orange juice but upon finishing breakfast, our friends declared that they were still hungry. Knowing exactly what they needed to fill up, the waiter was called over and an order was placed for molletes. In just a few minutes, a delicious platter of bubbling molletes was delivered to our table. Our friends finished them off and then said the molletes were so good they wanted more. We called the waiter over and placed still yet another order.

By now, the waiter looked at us kind of funny. After twenty minutes, we thought it strange that the molletes had not arrived. Happening to glance out the window, we saw our waiter running down the street.

Our Mexican friend, Eduardo, said the waiter ran away because he thought he was next if the cook ran out of molletes. We never did get the second order of molletes.

1 tablespoon olive oil (Mexican cooks would use lard here)
1 and 1/2 cups cooked beans
*   or canned refried beans*
About 1 and 1/2 cups grated white cheese
*   I like Monterey Jack and Kasseri*
3 bolillos or French rolls, split

1. If you are using the Frijoles Charros for the beans, heat the olive oil and add 1/2 cup beans and 1/2 cup liquid. Bring to a simmer and mash the beans with a large spoon or bean masher. When the beans and liquid are really thick, add another 1/2 cup beans and more liquid. Mash again. All the pieces of bacon, tomato, and serrano chile will add more flavor. When the beans are very thick, add the last 1/2 cup beans and about 1/4 cup liquid. Simmer and mash until thickened enough to spread on bolillos.

2. On top of each split bolillo, spread about 1/4 cup mashed beans. Sprinkle on 1/4 cup grated cheese.

3. Place molletes on a baking sheet and broil until the cheese is bubbly. Serve immediately.

Serves 6

MEXICAN BOLILLOS

One of the greatest gifts Maximilian and Carlota inno-
cently left to Mexico following their tragic three-year
reign in the 1860's was their appetite for European-style
pastries and breads. French-style breads were baked for
the homesick emperor and his entourage. Along came
the crusty rolls, known in Mexico as bolillos (little bob-
bins). Long after the demise of Max and the retreat of
his French army, the crusty breads and pastries remained
and became a part of Mexico's eclectic cuisine. Many
people think that tortillas are the only bread of Mexico
but bolillos are enthusiastically consumed along with
tortillas in every village and city of Mexico.

You can substitute Italian rolls for bolillos if you are
making molletes or tortas. But you won't catch me
admitting that they are the same. Bolillos are sweeter
and there is a infinitesimal something that is unique
about them. The exact right flavor had eluded me until I
discovered that Mexican bakers often put a big pinch of
cinnamon in their bolillo dough. Cinnamon is native to
Mexico so it is only natural to assume that back in the
1860's when some royal henchman demanded French
bread, the Mexican baker accommodated and then added
his own spice.

Also the wheat grown in Mexico, often used for flour
tortillas, is not as hard as our wheat so it works best to
use a combination of bread flour (sold in supermarkets
as high protein flour) and all-purpose flour to approxi-
mate real Mexican bolillos.

MEXICAN BOLILLOS (HARD ROLLS)

2 tablespoons sugar
2 and 1/2 cups warm water (105 to 108 degrees)
1 tablespoon active dry yeast
1 cup high protein bread flour
1 cup all-purpose, unbleached flour

1. Stir together the above ingredients to form a sponge. Allow the sponge to work for 1 hour undisturbed, covered with a damp towel or plastic wrap. Next add:

1 tablespoon salt
1 tablespoon very soft butter or shortening
1/2 teaspoon cinnamon
2 cups bread flour
1 and 1/2 cups all-purpose, unbleached flour
1/2 cup all-purpose, unbleached flour to stir in after
 machine kneading
1/2 cup water mixed with 2 teaspoons salt for misting
Plant mister

2. To the bowl of sponge add salt, butter, cinnamon, 2 cups bread flour, and 1 1/2 cups all-purpose, unbleached flour. Using the dough hook on your mixer, beat the dough for 4 minutes. If you do not have a strong mixer with a dough hook, knead the dough by hand for at least 10 minutes.

3. Stir in the last 1/2 cup of flour and knead by hand

for another 2 minutes, adding no more than another 1/2 of flour to the board.

4. Wash out bowl and grease with shortening. Place in the dough and turn once to coat. Cover and allow dough to rise for 1 hour.

5. Punch dough down and pull off 15 pieces of dough and form into balls. Roll them into oblong shapes about 4 inches long. Use your fingers to pull the ends into tapered points. Place bolillos on lightly greased, heavy baking sheets. Let them rise until doubled, about 30 minutes. Slash the bolillos across the tops lengthwise. Place salted water in plant mister. Gently mist bolillos before placing in oven.

6. Bake in a preheated 400 degree F. oven for 10 minutes. Then turn oven down to 375 degrees F. and bake for 20 more minutes or until bolillos are golden. If you want them to be particularly crusty, mist them 2 or 3 times more while they are baking. Eat them on baking day or wrap in foil and freeze. Bake them again in a 350 degree oven for 5 to 8 minutes to recrisp. Once they are placed in plastic bags the crusts will soften.

Makes 12 large bolillos.

PINEAPPLE MELON CONSERVE

You could drop some people in the middle of a foreign city and within minutes they would find the best place to eat, language being no barrier where the stomach is concerned. My friend Rocky Behr, who owns The Folk Tree in Pasadena, is one of those people and she is a master at finding the best breakfast. Recently, during a trip to Mexico City, her sixth sense directed her to the Jardín Prendes where she fell in love with a pineapple-melon conserve over freshly baked bolillos. From her description, I created this for her and now we too have fallen in love with it. The color of sunshine, it is one of the most lucious combinations of fruit.

2 cups finely diced fresh pineapple
1 cup sugar
1 cup diced cantaloupe
1 cup diced papaya (medium ripe but still firm)
A scant 1 cup sugar
2 strips lemon zest
2 strips orange zest
Juice of 1 lemon
Juice of 1 orange

1. Combine pineapple and 1 cup sugar. Simmer on low heat for 10 minutes.

2. To the pineapple, now add the cantaloupe, papaya, rest of sugar, lemon and orange zests, lemon and orange juices. Cook over medium heat until conserve is thick and fruit becomes clear and translucent. This takes about 20 minutes. Do not cook any longer as the conserve will thicken quite a bit when its is cooled and refrigerated.

3. Pour conserve into clean glass jar. It will keep for several weeks. Makes about 2 cups. Serve with toasted bolillos, toast, or English muffins.

BREAKFAST TORTAS

Another great use for bolillos is to make one of Mexico's most dearly loved sandwiches—tortas. They consume mountains of tortas for breakfast, lunch, and snacks.
Pull out some of the insides from bolillos or Italian rolls and stuff them with a variety of fillings. Improvise.
Mexican grocery stores usually carry fresh bolillos or make your own for tortas.

FILLINGS FOR TORTAS

Scrambled eggs and chorizo
Scrambled eggs with salsa verde
Scrambled eggs and red salsa
A thin layer of refried beans and
   Rings of pickled jalapeño chile
Slices of mild cheese like queso fresco or Monterey Jack
Crisp bacon or ham

1. Hollow out the bolillos to make room for fillings, reserving the breadcrumbs for another use.   Heat bolillos in a 350 degree F. oven until hot.

2. Using a spoon, spread a thin layer of warm refried beans on the inside of one half bolillo. Next add 1 of the above versions of scrambled eggs. Spread a thin layer of beans on the other half bolillo and lay in some slices of pickled jalapeño and cheese. You can actually pile in as many layers as you desire. Eat immediately or wrap in foil and carry to a breakfast picnic. These are a popular street food sold by the torta vendors in Mexico City.

PAN DULCE CHOCOLATE

When I first went to Mexico I was overwhelmed by the number of bakeries because I did not associate Mexican cuisine with pastries. The culinary extravagance of Maximilian and Carlota had left a lasting contribution-pastries, baroque with colored sugars, sprinkles and icings. Mexican cooks added their own touch to European pastries and I must admit that some of the most delicious pastries I have ever eaten have been in the elegant Zona Rosa of Mexico City.

The first time you visit a large panadería in Mexico you can be overwhelmed by the more than 100 types of pan dulce with all varieties of icing. A particular favorite is the shocking Mexican pink frosting. The pan dulce below is an Americanized version of the traditional which often has twice as many egg yolks as given in recipe below.

The little breads, cakelike and adorned with a scrumptious chocolate topping, make a perfect breakfast with coffee and fruit.

1 package active dry yeast or 3/4 tablespoon
  active dry yeast
1 teaspoon sugar
1/4 cup warm water
1/2 cup warm milk
2 teaspoons vanilla
1/2 cup sugar
1/3 cup soft unsalted butter

4 eggs, room temperature
1 teaspoon salt
4 and 1/2 cups unbleached, all-purpose flour

1. In a large mixing bowl dissolve yeast and sugar in the warm water (105-108 degrees). Proof for 10 minutes or until puffy.

2. To the bowl containing yeast mixture, add warm milk (108 degrees), vanilla, sugar, and eggs one at a time. Beat mixture until eggs are well-blended.

3. Next add 1 cup flour, salt, and the soft butter. Make sure that everything is well-blended and then add the rest of the flour-about 3 and 1/2 cups. Knead the soft dough on a well-floured board for about 5 minutes or until smooth. It will be sticky at first and kneading may be easier if you also use a dough scraper to help turn the dough.

4. Wash out the mixing bowl and rub with butter. Place in the kneaded dough and turn to coat with butter. Allow it to rise until doubled, about 1 to 1 and 1/2 hours. Meanwhile, make the chocolate topping:

CHOCOLATE TOPPING FOR PAN DULCE

3 ounces semi-sweet chocolate, melted
2 tablespoons butter
1 and 1/2 tablespoons flour
3 tablespoons powdered sugar
1 egg yolk blended with 1 tablespoon water
  for glazing pan dulce

1. Combine melted chocolate, butter, flour, and powdered sugar. Place in a bowl and freeze for 30 minutes until well-chilled. Process into chocolate crumbs in a food processor and place crumbs on a plate.

2. After the sweet dough has doubled, push it down and pinch off 12 pieces of dough to form the buns. Form the characteristic round shapes by first making a flat ball and turning all the edges under toward the bottom center. Brush buns with the water-yolk glaze, turn the flat bun upside down into the plate of chocolate crumbs and press so the whole top is covered with chocolate.   Place on greased baking sheet and continue forming the remainder.

3. Allow the pan dulce to rise 30 minutes. Bake in a preheated 375 degree F. oven for 12 to 15 minutes, just until golden. Do not overbake as the bread is delicate.

VANILLA TOPPING FOR PAN DULCE

This is the more traditional Mexican topping for pan dulce in which different designs, such as the spiral, are made on the surface of the breads. Mexican bakers usually have a collection of molds for creating various designs with the toppings.

2/3 cup all-purpose flour
1/2 cup sugar
1/2 teaspoon cinnamon
1 teaspoon vanilla
1/4 cup butter, melted
2 egg yolks

1. Mix the flour, sugar, cinnamon, vanilla, butter, and yolks together. You can leave the mixture crumbly and press the tops of each roll into it after glazing with egg yolk and water. Or you can divide the mixture into 12 portions and form into balls. Roll each ball into a circle that will fit over the top of each flattened pan dulce. Using the tip of a knife make shell designs or cross hatch designs.

2. Allow the pan dulce to rise for about 30 minutes. Bake in a preheated 375 degree oven for 15 minutes or until rolls are golden.

BREAD PUDDING WITH PAN DULCE

Nothing is ever wasted in a Mexican household and so something must always be done with the leftover pan dulce that may be a couple of days old. Bread pudding has almost all the same ingredients as French toast so why not eat it for breakfast?

3 cups crumbled, stale pan dulce or egg bread
1 quart milk
3 eggs, beaten
1/2 cup sugar
1/4 cup brown sugar
2 teaspoons vanilla
1/2 cup raisins
1/2 teaspoon cinnamon

1. Butter a 13 x 9 baking dish and fill with crumbled pan dulce.

2. Beat the milk, eggs, sugar, brown sugar, and vanilla until thoroughly combined. Stir in the raisins and cinnamon. Pour this mixture over the pan dulce.

3. Fill a larger, deep roasting pan with an inch of hot water and lower in the dish of pudding. This baño de María will help the pudding cook evenly.

4. Bake in a preheated 350 degree F. oven for 45 minutes or until pudding is almost set. Cool slightly before serving and cut into squares. Makes 8 servings. In Mexico this is served with a decadent pool of crema Mexicana, a thick, sweet cream akin to creme fraiche.

But you can eat the bread pudding just as it is or if not with cream, with lemon sauce or caramel sauce (see recipe for Aunt Anna's Caramel Sauce) and then it would be like eating dessert for breakfast.

FOR A VERY SUCCULENT PUDDING YOU CAN SUBSTITUTE HALF AND HALF FOR THE RE-QUIRED AMOUNT OF MILK.

CREMA DE ARROZ

A good friend of ours became very ill and confined to his bed for several weeks while living in Mexico. His maid fed him té de manzanilla (chamomile tea), paper thin slices of toasted bolillo, and rice cream for breakfast. He was a farm boy from Kansas and said he felt very sinful eating off a tray in bed and was glad his mother couldn't see him. When his strength miraculously returned and he could work again, he still ate rice cream for breakfast several mornings a week. It is less rich than rice pudding as it doesn't contain eggs and it is wonderfully soothing.

1 cup short-grain rice (like Calrose)
2 cups boiling water
1/2 teaspoon salt
5 cups milk (whole or low-fat)
1 tablespoon butter
3/4 cup sugar
2 cinnamon sticks, 3-inches long
1 piece vanilla bean, 2-inches long
Cinnamon powder for sprinkling
Plumped raisins, optional

1. Place rice in colander and rinse in cold water.   Bring 2 cups water to a boil in saucepan and add   rice. Simmer for 10 minutes. Drain rice in   colander.

2. Simmering the rice in a very heavy saucepan is helpful as then the rice takes care of itself except for an occasional stir and cooks more quickly than if you placed it in a double boiler. I use a 3-quart Calphalon saucepan to

simmer the rice, milk, butter, sugar, cinnamon sticks, and vanilla bean. First simmer over medium heat and then turn to low, cooking approximately 40 minutes. For the first 20 minutes, it will look like nothing is happening. Then suddenly the rice will begin to thicken and a wonderful cream will begin collecting on top. This is the combination of the starch of the rice blending with the milk, creating its own cream.

3. The Crema de Arroz will be thick enough in about 40 minutes. It will thicken more as it cools and is refrigerated. It is delicious served warm and sprinkled with more cinnamon. You can add plump raisins if you like.

Makes 6 servings.

SHORT GRAIN RICE CONTAINS MORE NATURAL STARCH AND SO WORKS BEST IN THIS RECIPE.

PLUMPED RAISINS

I almost feel silly giving instructions for this utterly simple task but these succulent raisins add such life to Crema de Arroz, baked apples, hot oatmeal, or even Grape Nuts I must give you the instructions. Cover 1 cup raisins with 1/2 cup water. Simmer on high power in a microwave oven for 60 seconds. Store the raisins in a glass jar in refrigerator to they are ready to sprinkle over pudding or cereal.

SWISS MEXICAN VANILLA YOGURT

It seems strange that it was in Mexico that I had my first taste of yogurt. The central highlands of Querétaro and Celaya where we lived for almost four years, was like the Wisconsin of Mexico. In the 1930's many Swiss and Germans immigrated to Mexico and gravitated to this area where there were many dairies and cheese making operations. In the village of San Juan del Río, we discovered a Swiss man who made extraordinary crema Chantilly (like creme fraiche) and yogurt. We drove forty miles every two or three weeks just to buy his wares. You could buy yogurt either plain, blended with fresh strawberries in the spring, or with vanilla. The pristine white yogurt was speckled with grains of vanilla bean and this was my favorite. Thinking back now on how creamy and mild the Swiss yogurt was, I suspect it was made with very rich milk and maybe some of the crema Chantilly. No wonder it was so good.

For years I have fussed with different yogurt makers which all seemed to produce acidic yogurt by the time it was properly thickened. Then I discovered yogurt can be easily made just in the warmth of a gas oven with a pilot light. I think that the overall warmth of the oven produces a less acidic yogurt than the bottom heat of many yogurt makers.

1 quart of 1 %, low-fat, or whole milk
1 /4 cup powdered milk
2 tablespoons plain, unpasteurized yogurt
  or 1 package (5 g.) dried yogurt culture
1 5-inch piece vanilla bean

1. Heat milk in pot over medium heat to 180 degrees F. Remove from heat and whisk in the powdered milk. Allow milk to cool down to 108 to 112 degrees F. I usually pour the milk back and forth in glass Pyrex pitchers to help it cool down more quickly. A Taylor thermometer is good for checking temperatures.

2. In separate little bowl beat some of the cooled milk into the yogurt culture and then pour back into the pitcher of milk, blending well. Using a sharp paring knife cut the vanilla bean in half and scrape out the moist grains. Whisk the vanilla grains into the milk.

3. Pour the warm milk into 4 clean glasses (I use French jelly glasses that come with plastic lids). Set glasses in a pan and place in oven with just the heat of the pilot. The yogurt should be thick enough in 3 to 4 hours depending upon your oven's warmth and whether it's winter or summer. In winter it seems to take longer—at least 4 hours. You can also pour yogurt into a wide-mouthed thermos that has been rinsed out with hot water. It will also take about 4 hours to thicken in the thermos. Also all yogurt thickens more when cooled in the refrigerator. I like to drizzle homemade vanilla yogurt over a plate of sliced fruits like cantaloupe, peaches, and strawberries.

4. Save a heaping tablespoon of your fresh yogurt as a starter for your next batch. After 3 or 4 times of using my own yogurt as a starter I use one of the dried yogurt cultures from the health food store. The Yogourmet, a freeze-dried starter, is excellent.

Makes 1 quart Swiss Mexican Vanilla Yogurt.

DO NOT BE TEMPTED TO USE MORE CULTURE
OR STARTER THAN 2 TABLESPOONS AS IT WILL
JUST MAKE YOUR YOGURT MORE ACIDIC.

MEXICAN HOT KAKES

Pancakes, commonly known as hot kakes in Mexico, and waffles have definitely made inroads into the Mexican breakfast. The first time I unexpectedly experienced them in Mexico, I had lived in San Miguel de Allende for several months and was particularly hungry for American food. It was the night between the Día de Los Muertos (Day of the Dead) and Día de Los Santos (All Saint's Day), November 1 and 2. Stalls selling sugar skulls and animals, toys, funeral candles and everything pertaining to the celebration of life and death were set up around the jardín. Women were cooking traditional foods over braziers.

One family had a stand that sold nothing but big, fluffy hot kakes and brown sugar syrup, tasting amazingly good on a cold morning at 2 AM.

2 cups all-purpose flour
2 tablespoons cornstarch
3 teaspoons baking powder
2 tablespoons sugar
3/4 teaspoon salt
3 eggs, beaten
1 and 1/2 cups milk
3 tablespoons melted butter
2 teaspoons vanilla

1. Sift dry ingredients together. Combine egg, milk, butter, and vanilla. Blend liquid and dry ingredients. Avoid overmixing so the Hot Kakes will be tender.

2. Pour 1/4 cup measure of batter on a hot greased griddle or in a large frying pan. Cook hot kakes until they have formed bubbles across the top and then turn.

Serves 4-6. Serve with syrup or jam.

CUT THIN SLICES OF MEDIUM RIPE BANANA AND STIR INTO THE BATTER FOR BANANA HOT KAKES. CHILDREN LOVE THEM THIS WAY.

CHOCOLATE OAXACAN STYLE

Chocolate was a staple in Mexico when the Spaniards arrived but at that time it was consumed only as a drink among royalty. Oaxacans still view chocolate as a beverage and offer it to guests as   something special-even on a warm day.

One of my favorite walks in Oaxaca is down the chocolate street where small shops sell tablets of chocolate and grind fresh chocolate beans with almonds, cinnamon, and crude sugar to your specification or family recipe. It is a very coarse and granular chocolate made just for drinking. Afterwards, you smell wonderful as you wander down the street with this warm, oozy chocolate bagged in plastic, ready to place in molds or form into tabletas.

The Mexicans wrap the tabletas in bright colors of tissue. When you want to serve a chocolate drink, you simmer a couple of tabletas with water and then whip it to a froth with a molinillo or a whisk. The richer the chocolate, the higher the fat content, and the greater the foam or espuma which is the valued part of the chocolate.

ANTIQUE RECIPE FOR OAXACAN CHOCOLATE

1 kilo de cacao beans tabasco (2 pounds)
3 onzas of blanched almonds (about 100 grams)
3 onzas of cinnamon (about 100 grams)
1 kilo sugar (about 2 pounds)

1. If you happen to be near one of the tiendas in Oaxaca where they grind chocolate to your specification, give them these measurements or half all of the above amounts. You can also buy tabletas of chocolate already made up. And if you are not going to Oaxaca in the near future, you can buy the Mexican brand of Ibarra chocolate in most supermarkets in the ethnic section.

2. To make the Oaxacan-style chocolate drink, simmer a cup of water per tablet for fairly thick chocolate. In Mexico, this is done in a clay pitcher but I use a deep saucepan so that the chocolate doesn't splatter when it is whisked or beat with a handheld blender. When it is foamy, pour into cups and serve immediately.

CAFE CON LECHE

This Mexican ritual, coffee with hot milk, makes our mornings. The main requirement for cafe con leche is that the coffee beans used should be a dark roast and the resulting coffee be made very strong or else it won't hold up to all the hot milk that is added. For each cup or glass of cafe con leche, pour in 1/2 cup strong coffee and fill up the cup with hot milk.

ORANGE LICUADO

Mexicans have healthy habits to balance out their love of sweets and one of our favorites are licuados or the drinks of pureed fruits mixed with other juices or milk. Below is one of our favorites.

1 can frozen orange juice (6 ounces)
1 cup ice water
Juice squeezed from 1 orange
8 ice cubes
1 cup low-fat or whole milk
1 teaspoon pure vanilla
1 orange cut into slices

1. In blender jar, place frozen juice, ice water, orange juice, ice, milk, and vanilla. Blend until frothy. Serve in tall glasses adorned with a slice of orange. These are great to accompany any breakfast.

Serves 4.

RAINBOW BATIDOS

Batidos are Cuban licuados (in Cuba, milk and sugar are typically added to blended fruit drinks). When guests are arriving for a brunch I like to serve these frosty drinks in beautiful, long-stemmed Spanish glasses.

1 and 1/2 cups fresh squeezed orange juice
1 cup bottled tropical juice
  (preferably pineapple and papaya)
1 cup frozen strawberries
1 cup frozen boysenberries or marionberries
3/4 cup low-fat or regular milk
2 tablespoons sugar
6 ice cubes

   1. Combine everything in a blender and whirl until frothy.

 Serves 6.

LICUADOS AND BATIDOS HELP COOL THE PAL-
ATE DURING SPICY MEXICAN BREAKFASTS.

CHAPTER II

BREAKFAST IN THE SOUTHWEST

Living in Mexico for almost five years preordained that we could never again accept life without Mexico for that would be like life without dessert. Like other Americans, we complained about the mañana complex and how difficult it was to get things done but when we returned to the hustle of the U.S. we sorely missed the kind of culture that took time for a small favor even if it meant being late and missing the bus out of town.

In Mexico aesthetics enters into the smallest detail of everyday life. The occupants of a thatched-roofed hut put tin cans filled with bright geraniums around their dirt yard; a shopkeeper wraps the biscochitos you buy in pink, red, and green tissue for a gift. The man in the local marketplace always arranges his oranges in a perfect pyramid. The lady selling eggs presents them in a basket lined with leaves.

These small attentions once received make one regret not having them. So when we are homesick for a slower pace, we make the trip, if not to Mexico, to Santa Fe and environs. We always find what we're looking for and are often surprised with what we're not looking for.

Santa Fe co-mingles its Indian past with ancient Spanish and Mexican customs, drawing from the color of its mixed past. It's not uncommon to walk into an adobe house, its coarse walls adorned with antique tapestries and fine Persian carpets thrown on rough terra cotta floors. Like Mexico, there is a blend of the delicate and the crude.

The cuisine of the Southwest is also the paradoxical combination of the delicate and the rough. The earthiest hot green chiles. Smooth bland atoles. Indian blue corn and cream. Fiery red chiles. Succulent chicken and quail. More attention to eating goes on in Santa Fe than almost anywhere else I've been (except maybe San Francisco and New Orleans).

And it starts off with a good breakfast. Recently, we were in Santa Barbara very early in the morning, starving hungry and we couldn't find anywhere to eat breakfast. That wouldn't have happened in Santa Fe. The real problem is being able to eat breakfast in all your favorite places in the few mornings you have in town. Santa Fe is a very breakfast town from the New Age restaurants where they try to "dress up" earthy Southwestern cooking to the old cafes where you meet worn cowboy boots and Levis coming in the door and you are reminded that Santa Fe is not just a tourist town.

The recipes included in this chapter will give you some of the spice of the Southwest back in your own kitchen sans cafe ambiance but you can still eat well and have your chile fix.

CHILE RELLENO OMELET

The crowning glory of the Southwest are the chiles, red and green. I plan my trips there by the chile seasons and never return home without arranging a shipment of chiles to my kitchen. Then I have to deal with 20 pounds all at once, meaning I get creative by necessity.

When I had leftover chiles rellenos, I discovered how great they were stuffed into the middle of omelets. If you do not have leftover rellenos, there's an easy way to fix them.

2 fresh green chiles, Anaheim or New Mexican
1/2 cup grated Monterey Jack or Cheddar cheese
5 eggs, lightly beaten
1 tablespoon butter
Salsa, recipe below

1. Char the green chiles over a flame until skin is blackened. Place in a bag for a couple of minutes so the skin will steam and loosen. Peel off the blackened skin under running water and pull out seeds. Blot chiles dry with paper towel and stuff with the grated cheese. Place chiles on baking sheet and bake for 10 minutes in a preheated 350 degree F. oven or until cheese is melted.

2. Next melt 1/2 tablespoon butter in a nonstick omelet pan. Pour in half the beaten eggs when the butter is sizzling but not brown. I use a 14-inch nonstick skillet so the beaten eggs spread out in a thin layer and are set up in under a minute. Use a spatula to lift up the omelet's edges to allow any remaining liquid egg to flow underneath. Keep moving skillet until omelet is set. Remove 1 chile relleno from oven and place in omelet. Fold over and slide omelet onto warm plate. Leave a stem of the chile sticking out for effect. Douse the omelet with warmed salsa (red or green). Serve with refried beans and tortillas. Makes 2 omelets.

MESQUITE SALSA

Mesquite Salsa is served by a popular grill in Newport Beach, California and the restaurant is constantly asked for the recipe which is actually very simple. The chefs grill the tomatoes and peppers over a mesquite-fired grill. They claim that they even barbecue the cilantro over mesquite but I think this is far-fetched. The trick is to add 1 or 2 canned chipotle chiles and that will give the mysterious "mesquite taste" that the chefs add. This fiery flavor of this salsa is particularly good with egg dishes like the Chile Relleno Omelet.

4 tomatoes
4 serrano chiles
1 to 2 chipotle chiles en adobo, from can
1 whole red onion
1 teaspoon salt
1 to 2 tablespoons cilantro, minced

1. Char the tomatoes, serrano chiles, and a whole red onion under a broiler, over a gas flame, or over a mesquite-fired grill. Turn vegetables frequently. This should take about 8 to 10 minutes.

2. Remove most of the blackened skins from the tomatoes but allow the chiles to retain bits of their charred skins for flavor. Place tomatoes, serrano chiles, chipotle chile, and 1/2 of red onion cut into pieces in the bowl of a food processor. Chop using an on and off pulsation.

3. Remove salsa to a saucepan and add the red onion, salt, and cilantro. If you want the salsa hotter you may add the second chipotle chile. Taste first as chipotle is very hot. Simmer for a couple of minutes to remove raw taste and bring the flavors together.

Makes about 2 cups salsa.

RED CHILE POTATOES IN A SKILLET

These were invented when I had leftover baked potates.
The next morning I diced and sauteed them with a bit of
onion, and doused them with red chile powder. It couldn't
be easier. This is the fastest way I know of doing breakfast
potatoes. You just have to think ahead and bake extra.
You can use these to accompany any breakfast (lunch or
dinner) or use to help fill a breakfast burrito.

2 extra large Russet potatoes, baked the day before
1 to 2 tablespoons canola or olive oil
1/2 cup diced red onion
1/2 teaspoon salt
2 to 4 teaspoons New Mexican chile powder (like Dixon)

1. Dice the potatoes, leaving on the skins, while the oil
is heating in a heavy skillet preferably cast-iron.

2. Throw in the onions and potatoes and saute for 10
minutes or until lightly browned. Add salt and chile powder. You can add more chile if you want the potatoes
really spicy. Saute for 5 more minutes but be careful as the
chile powder can burn.

Serves 3 to 4 as a side dish.

SANTA FE BREAKFAST BURRITO

Everywhere you go for breakfast in Santa Fe, you seem to find some form of the breakfast burrito. The Red Chile Potatoes above are perfect to combine with scrambled eggs in a burrito. Breakfast burritos are slathered either in the ubiquitous red chile sauce, green chile sauce, or salsa.

RED CHILE RANCHERO SAUCE

8 dried New Mexican red chiles
1/2 pound plum tomatoes
1/2 cup chopped red onion
4 cloves unpeeled garlic
1 cup water or chicken broth
2 teaspoons vinegar
1 teaspoon toasted cumin seed
1 teaspoon salt

_____

1 recipe of Red Chile Potatoes in a Skillet, see above
1 tablespoon oil
6 eggs
4 burrito size flour tortillas
2 cups grated Monterey Jack cheese

1. First make Red Chile Ranchero Sauce, preferably the night before. Toast the chiles on a baking sheet in a pre-heated 350 degree F. oven for 4 to 5 minutes. Do not burn. When chiles are cool rinse them off in cold water and place in a bowl. Cover with boiling water and allow chiles to steep for an hour.

2. Meanwhile, broil the tomatoes and unpeeled garlic for about 10 minutes. Toast the cumin seeds in a skillet for a couple of minutes.

3. Place the soaked chiles in a food processor along with tomatoes and garlic. Puree and then push through a sieve into a saucepan. Add the chopped red onion, vinegar, salt, and toasted cumin. Simmer sauce for 10 to 15 minutes to remove raw taste and concentrate flavors.

4. Beat the eggs lightly. Heat the oil in a skillet and scramble the eggs. Stir in the Red Chile Potatoes. Warm the tortillas just until pliable on a comal or griddle.

5. Lay out the warm tortilla. Place about 3/4 cup of the potato-scrambled egg mixture down the middle. Add some cheese. Fold down the ends and fold over the sides. Place burrito on plate and drizzle Red Chile Ranchero Sauce over the top. You can also sprinkle some of the grated cheese over tops of burritos.

THESE BURRITOS ARE RELATIVELY EASY TO MAKE IF YOU HAVE MADE UP THE RANCHERO SAUCE THE DAY BEFORE AND YOU HAVE LEFT-OVER BAKED POTATOES.

STACKED REDS WITH POACHED EGGS

Traditional New Mexican enchiladas are not rolled as they are in Mexico but left flat and stacked. One or two poached or fried eggs can be placed on top, justifying them as a perfect breakfast for hearty eaters. On our California rancho, red enchiladas left from the day before were always savored for breakfast with an egg.

2 tablespoons canola oil
18 blue corn or regular corn tortillas
3 cups of cooked pinto beans or Frijoles Charros
3 cups grated Cheddar cheese
2 and 1/2 cups Red Chile Ranchero Sauce, see recipe above
1 to 2 fried or poached eggs per stacked enchilada

1. Fry each tortilla in hot oil just until softened and crisp around the edges. Dip in red sauce and lay on jelly roll pan or oven-proof plates. For the filling for each stack use 1/4 cup beans and 1/4 cup grated cheese. Place another softened and dipped tortilla on top. Add another layer of beans and cheese. Add the third fried and dipped tortilla. Sprinkle top with a tablespoon of cheese. You have now completed 1 stacked enchilada. Construct the other 5 enchiladas.

2. Place in hot 350 degree F. oven for 8 to 10 minutes or just long enough to melt cheese. Pull out and place each stack on a plate. Place a fried egg on top.

Makes 6 Stacked Reds. Serve immediately.

ROGER HAYOT'S PAN DE MAIZ
WITH CHIPOTLE SAUCE AND EGGS

Roger, who is the chef-owner of the Authentic Cafe in Los Angeles deserves the title, King of the Chipotles, because he loves these potent chiles so much he keeps trying to think up more ways of using them.

Sometimes he substitutes the moras and morita chiles, which are a type of smoked red jalapeño, for the traditional chipotles. The flavors are almost identical except the mora seems to have a brighter less dusky flavor.

The combination of the hot chipotle sauce over the sweet cornbread and eggs makes one of the best breakfasts I can think of.

PAN DE MAIZ (CORNBREAD)

I adapted this from one of Marion Cunningham's breakfast recipes for corn muffins and it makes a very light, sweet pan de maiz that is perfect to serve as the base for the eggs and chipotle sauce. Since Roger's recipe has three parts it is best to make the pan de maiz first.

1/4 cup butter, melted
1/4 cup canola oil
1 cup low-fat or whole milk, warmed
1 egg, room temperature
1 cup cake flour
1 tablespoon baking powder (preferably non-aluminum type)
2/3 cup yellow cornmeal
3 tablespoon sugar
1/2 teaspoon salt

1. Preheat oven to 400 degrees F. Oil a 9 x 13-inch baking dish.

2. Combine butter, oil, milk, and egg in mixing bowl and whisk until well- blended.

3. Stir the flour, baking powder, cornmeal, sugar, and salt together with a fork until well-mixed. To this dry mixture, add the liquid milk mixture and stir just until combined.

4. Pour into baking dish. Bake the cornbread until golden on top and a tester inserted in the middle comes out clean. Baking time is about 25 minutes.

Hint: if you are in a hurry you can use Jiffy cornbread mix (8 and 1/2 ounce size). To the dry mix, add 1/2 cup evaporated milk, 1 egg, and 1 tablespoon melted butter in place of what is called for on the package. Bake at 400 degrees F. for 20 minutes. Bread should be golden brown and a tester plunged into its middle should have no batter clinging to it.

CHIPOTLE SAUCE

1 tablespoon olive oil
2 tablespoons shallots, minced
1 tablespoon flour
1/2 teaspoon dried sage
1 teaspoon dried thyme
1 to 2 dried chipotles or mora chiles, reconstituted
1 and 2/3 cups chicken broth
1/2 cup cream
Salt to taste

1. Before you begin preparing everything else, pour boiling water over 2 dried chipotle or mora chiles. Allow them to soak (covered) for at least an hour and when they are well softened, puree them in a food processor with 1/4 cup water or chicken broth.

2. Meanwhile, sauté shallots in olive oil until softened. Then add flour and cook just until lightly brown. Stir in the herbs and slowly whisk in the chicken broth. Simmer for 5 minutes and then add the cream.

3. Simmer sauce for 15 minutes or until slightly reduced. Cream will thicken. Next add 2 teaspoons of the chipotle puree. Simmer for 5 more minutes to concentrate flavors. If you want more chipotle flavor, you may add more puree at this point. Be careful, it's picante.

4. Poach or lightly fry 2 eggs per person. This recipe makes enough cornbread and sauce for 6 people so you will need to prepare 12 eggs.

5. Cut cornbread into 6 large squares. Put a square on each plate. Place soft-cooked eggs on top of cornbread and ladle on about 1/3 cup of Chipotle Sauce per serving. These eggs are great accompanied by black beans, Turkey-Jalapeño Cilantro Sausage and a side of chopped fruit to cool down the palate.

Serves 6.

RESERVE LEFTOVER CHIPOTLE PUREE FOR ANOTHER RECIPE. OR BLEND WITH OLIVE OIL OR MAYONAISE AND DASH OF LIME JUICE. USE AS A SANDWICH SPREAD. MAKES DYNAMITE GRILLED CHEESE SANDWICHES.

TURKEY JALAPEÑO CILANTRO SAUSAGE

This healthy, savory sausage is a beautiful chile color flecked with the green of cilantro and jalapeños. This sausage is made in heaven to accompany Southwestern or Mexican breakfasts. It is quite easy to make if you have a food processor with a sharp blade or a sausage grinding attachment for your mixer. Extra sausage can be frozen in patties which can be later sauteed and added to beans, rice dishes like paella, and to accompany spicy breakfasts. A patty of this sausage and a fried egg wedged into an English muffin will make the best McMuffin you've ever had. Or bake the Pan de Maiz (recipe given above) into small muffins, split them and fill with a patty of Turkey Jalapeño Cilantro Sausage.

1 pound boned turkey thigh meat (skin removed)
1/2 pound boned turkey breast meat (skin removed)
1/2 pound packaged turkey pork sausage
1/4 cup white wine or white zinfandel
2 minced jalapeño chiles, reserve some seeds
1/2 cup minced cilantro
1 teaspoon sugar
2 teaspoons salt
1/2 teaspoon freshly ground black pepper
1 and 1/2 tablespoons ground New Mexican chile,
   (like Dixon chile)
1 teaspoon ground dried chipotle chile (optional)

1. Large supermarkets usually sell 2 turkey thighs to a package. When boned, they equal about a pound. Just use a small, sharp knife to cut against the bone to remove the

thigh meat. Usually breast meat is sold already boned.
Cut all of the thigh and breast meat into small chunks and
freeze in a plastic bag for a hour. In three batches, finely
chop the partially frozen meat in your food processor. It
should have the texture of hamburger. If you are using a
sausage grinder attachment, you do not have to partially
freeze the meat.

2. Place the ground turkey in a large bowl and add half
the package of turkey pork sausage (this serves as a
binder). Next add the wine, chiles and their reserved
seeds, cilantro, and seasonings. Mix with your hands or a
large spoon until all of the ingredients are well-blended.
Cover bowl with plastic wrap and chill for at least an hour
before using so the flavors have a chance to blend.

3. To use your homemade sausage, just form 3-inch
patties. Add a tablespoon of canola oil to a large nonstick
skillet and sauté sausage patties over medium low heat for
about ten minutes. Turn frequently and watch as the red
chile can cause the sausage to brown quickly.

Serves 8.

YOU CAN FREEZE EXTRA SAUSAGE BY FORMING
PATTIES AND PLACING BETWEEN LAYERS OF
WAXED PAPER. KEEPS FOR A MONTH.

LOW CHOLESTEROL GREEN CHILE FRITTATA

What I truly like about a frittata is that there is a greater percentage of filling as opposed to egg. Be creative with this frittata and add things that you like: a little bit of minced Canadian bacon, minced spinach, grated zucchini, or some of the Red Chile Potatoes (recipe given above). If you are on a low cholesterol diet and cannot eat any egg yolks, simply use enough egg substitute (2 ounces) to equal 1 egg in addition to the egg whites.

Olive oil spray or 1 teaspoon olive oil
1/4 cup chopped red onion
1/2 cup sliced red bell pepper
  or the Italian red peppers found in jars
1/2 cup chopped green chile (charred, skinned, seeded)
1 whole egg
4 egg whites
1/2 teaspoon salt (optional)
1/4 teaspoon freshly ground pepper
1 teaspoon ground red chile (New Mexican like Dixon)
1 tablespoon snipped cilantro
1/2 cup to 3/4 cup reduced fat Cheddar cheese

   1. Place the olive oil in a 10-inch nonstick skillet and heat. Sauté the onion until softened, about 5 minutes. Then add the red bell pepper and green chile and sauté also.

   2. Beat the egg whites until foamy and then add the whole egg (or egg substitute) and beat. Add salt, pepper, red chile, and cilantro. Pour the egg mixture on top of the vegetable mixture in the skillet.

3. Cook the frittata on low heat until almost set. You may place a lid on top of the pan to help. Sprinkle on cheese just before the frittata is done.
To serve, cut the frittata in triangles and lift from skillet with spatula.

Serves 2.

ME AND PASQUAL'S POTATOES

One of my favorite Santa Fe breakfasts are the papas fritas served at Pasqual's. This recipe, an adaptation of Pasqual's, is also in my *Red And Green Chile Cookbook* but I must include it here also for fear that someone might miss having them. After all these aren't just potatoes, they are an institution.

12 to 14 red new potatoes, scrubbed
2 tablespoons canola or olive oil
1 cup grated Monterey Jack cheese
6 green onions, minced
3/4 cup sour cream (you can use reduced fat)
Red Chile Gravy (see recipe below)
4 Fried Eggs to top each bowl of potatoes

1. Steam potatoes until done (25 minutes). This can be done the night before breakfast.

2. When cool enough to handle, slice and chop the potatoes.

3. Add oil to a heavy skillet, preferably cast-iron, frying potatoes until they are golden, about 10 to 15 minutes. While the potatoes are frying, you can stir up the Red Chile Gravy.

4. This recipe only serves 4 people because everyone eats so much of the potatoes. Fill 4 wide soup bowls with potatoes and drizzle with 1/4 cup Red Chile Gravy (but they'll want more). Next sprinkle on some cheese, green onions, and a dollop of sour cream. On top of all this you can precariously balance a fried egg which is sort of anti-climactic but you might as well gild the chile.

Serves 4 hearty eaters.

RED CHILE GRAVY

2 tablespoons canola oil
1 tablespoon butter
2 tablespoons flour
1/4 teaspoon ground cumin
Scant 1/2 cup ground New Mexican red chile
  (Dixon is a favorite)
1 cup cold water
2 and 1/2 cups chicken broth or vegetable stock
1 clove garlic, minced through a press
1 teaspoon salt

1. Heat the oil, stirring in flour and cook until a golden color. Add cumin powder. Slowly blend the cold water into the red chile until there are no lumps. Remove the skillet from the heat and blend in the red chile. Put back on heat and slowly whisk in the broth. Simmer for 20 minutes, adding the garlic and salt. If chile gravy becomes too thick, thin out with broth or water. Serve over the potatoes or enchiladas or burritos.

TORTITAS WITH RED CHILE SAUCE

These little puffs of egg are served both in Mexico and the Southwest and are a perfect way to eat more red chile sauce. For this recipe you can also use the Red Chile Gravy given with Pasqual's Potatoes but Las Palmas or the Santa Cruz Chili Paste is good when you haven't much time to spare.

4 eggs, separated
2 tablespoons all-purpose flour or cornmeal
  (yellow or blue)
Pinch of salt
2 green onions, finely minced
2 cups canola oil for frying puffs

RED CHILE SAUCE

1 tablespoon oil
1 tablespoon flour
1 can (10 ounces) red chile sauce like Las Palmas
Pinch of ground cumin
1 teaspoon vinegar

1. First make the sauce by browning the flour in the oil until golden. Whisk in the red chile sauce, cumin, and vinegar and simmer for 10 minutes.

2. Separate the eggs. Beat the yolks with flour, salt, and green onions.

3. Beat the egg whites until they form soft peaks. Gently fold in the egg yolk mixture.

4. Drop the egg batter by tablespoons into the hot oil. When tortitas are golden on one side, turn over. As each puff is cooked, lift with slotted spoon and drain on paper towels. As they cool the puffs will deflate.

5. Just before serving, reheat the Red Chile Sauce and add the tortitas. Simmer gently with lid on for a few minutes. The contained heat will cause the tortitas to souffle again. Serve immediately.

Serves 4 as a main dish but 6 as a side dish.

SALSA EGGS IN RAMEKINS

I usually have leftover homemade salsa and always feel wiser when I pull it out like some hidden treasure. Spoon salsa into porcelain ramekins and cook eggs in one of the easiest ways known to the cook. Green salsa is one of our favorites for this recipe.

1 tablespoon butter
1/4 cup minced green onions
1/2 cup minced green chile
2 tablespoon balsamic vinegar
2 cups red or green salsa
6 eggs
6 heat-proof custard cups or ramekins

1. Preheat oven to 375 degrees. Butter ramekins and sprinkle each one with a little green onion and green chile. Over this sprinkle a couple teaspoons of balsamic.

2. Carefully crack an egg over the top of the green chile mixture. Spoon 1/3 cup salsa around each egg.

3. Place filled dishes on baking sheet and bake for 8 to 10 minutes, depending upon how firm you want the eggs.

Remove dishes and place on dinner plates. Serve with warm tortillas.

CRUMBLE FRIED CHORIZO OR TURKEY JALAPEÑO CILANTRO SAUSAGE AROUND THE EDGES OF EGGS BEFORE BAKING FOR A CREATIVE TOUCH.

GREEN CHILE SPOON BREAD

A combination of cornmeal, eggs, and chiles makes for an easy and comforting breakfast or brunch. Spoonbread, a cross between custard and cornbread, complements spicy food perfectly.

1 cup cornmeal
2 cups boiling water
1 teaspoon salt
1 ear of corn, kernels removed
1 large green poblano chile, Anaheim
   or New Mexican green chile
4 tablespoons butter
4 beaten eggs
1 and 1/2 cups milk

1. Roast the chile over a flame or under a broiler until skin is blackened. Steam chile in paper bag or plastic bag for 5 minutes to loosen skin. Remove blackened skin, core, and seeds. Dice chile and set aside.

2. Slowly add cornmeal to saucepan of the boiling water and salt. Simmer gently for 2 minutes.

3. Remove from heat and add butter, corn kernels, and chile.

4. Let cool slightly and then beat in eggs and milk.

5. Butter a 2-quart casserole or souffle dish and pour in the spoonbread. Bake in a preheated 375 degree oven for about 45 to 50 minutes. Top should be puffed and golden brown.

Serves 4

STUFFED AND MARINATED JALAPEÑOS

When you are serving brunch it is nice to entice your guests with little surprises and these have become a standby. We love them any time of day.

1 small can of flamed jalapeño chiles (unpickled)
1 tablespoon olive oil
1/2 cup cider vinegar
1 clove minced garlic
1/2 teaspoon salt
****
1/2 cup crumbled mild goat cheese
2 teaspoons mayonnaise
1 tablespoon plain yogurt
1 tablespoon minced cilantro
2 teaspoons of above marinade
Cilantro leaves to garnish tops of filled chiles

1. Carefully half each jalapeño chile and place in marinade for several hours or overnight.

2. Blend the goat cheese, mayonnaise, yogurt, cilantro, and enough of marinade to the the mixture nice and moist.

3. Use a small spoon to place the filling in each jalapeño half. Garnish each chile half with a cilantro leaf. You can serve immediately or hold for several hours before serving.

Makes about 14 filled chile halves.

JICAMA PANCAKES

One of the results of loving to eat is being ready to try anything, even Jicama Pancakes. I played around with Chef Dean Fearing's Jicama Hash Browns until I came up with a slightly lightened version made into little crisp pancakes that I could serve with a spicy breakfast.

Jicama is a Mexican root vegetable with a skin resembling a Russet potato. A crisp, white interior is revealed inside once the tough brown skin is peeled off. Mexicans routinely eat jicama wedges sprinkled with lime juice and ground hot chile for snacks.

3 cups shredded jicama
Juice of 1 lemon
1 tablespoon snipped chives
1 egg, beaten
1 tablespoon flour
1/2 teaspoon salt
2 teaspoon ground red chile
3 tablespoons canola oil

1. Peel off the outer brown layer of the jicama. Shred using a big-holed grater. Squeeze lemon juice over jicama and drain in colander for 15 minutes and then use your hands to squeeze out more moisture. It is loaded with water. Place shredded jicama in a bowl and blot with paper towels.

2. Mix shredded jicama with chives, flour, egg, salt, and chile powder.

3. Heat 2 tablespoons oil in nonstick skillet. Form the jicama mixture into little 2-inch patties and sauté several at a time in the skillet. Brown them on one side and then turn. Add the third tablespoon of canola oil if needed. They should be crisp and brown on outside and creamy on inside.

Makes about 10 to 12 jicama pancakes to accompany any Mexican or Southwestern breakfast.

POLENTA CORN CAKES

The polenta can be made the night before serving time. Once during a cooking class at the Santa Fe School of Cooking, we went through an alarming number of these. We were sautéeing corn cakes as fast as people could eat them.

The secret to good polenta is to add the cornmeal slowly and cook it for about 25 minutes so that the grains are thoroughly cooked.

4 cups water
1 can low fat evaporated milk plus
  enough water to make 2 cups liquid
1 teaspoon salt
1 and 1/2 cups polenta cornmeal
1 shallot, minced finely
3 teaspoons butter
1/3 cup freshly grated Parmesan or Asiago cheese
1 to 2 tablespoons olive oil for sauteing

1. Lightly butter or rub a 9 x 13-inch baking dish with olive oil. In a large, heavy bottomed saucepan combine water, the milk-water combination, and salt. Bring to a boil and slowly sprinkle in the cornmeal while stirring at the same time. Stir and sprinkle. Lumps will form if you add the polenta too fast. Stir constantly with a big spoon for 15 minutes. Toward the last 2 minutes, add the minced shallots.

2. Remove polenta from heat. Stir in the butter. Pour polenta into the buttered dish. Sprinkle the cheese over the

surface and use a spoon to barely stir cheese into the top. If the cheese remains more on the top, it will help the polenta to brown when it is sautéed.

3. Allow the polenta to set up for 30 minutes at room temperature or store well-covered in the refrigerator overnight.

4. Cut polenta into 3-inch squares. Sauté in batches, in hot olive oil, until golden and crusty on both sides. Everyone fights over the ones that have been overly browned. You may need to add more olive oil to the pan. Serve immediately after browning as this is when the cakes are at their creamiest and very best.

Makes 20 3-inch Polenta Corn Cakes.

GLAZED BACON

Years ago the late James Beard rhapsodized in one of his columns about this marvelous, almost candied bacon that Betty Groff served in her Pennsylvania inn. If you only eat bacon once a year or on special occasions, you should make it Glazed Bacon. It is good even when it has cooled and it is marvelous snipped into spinach or chicken salads.

1/2 pound meaty bacon
1/3 cup brown sugar
2 teaspoons jalapeño mustard or Dijon mustard
2 tablespoons frozen apple juice concentrate, thawed
   (James Beard called for wine here)

1. Lay the bacon strips out on a large jelly roll pan. Bake in a preheated 350 degree oven for 10 minutes to render fat. Pour off collected fat.

2. Mix brown sugar, mustard, and apple juice together and spread half of mixture over the tops of the bacon. Return to oven for 8 minutes. Then turn bacon over and cover with remaining sugar mixture. Bake until golden, about 8 more minutes, but watch carefully so bacon does not become too dark. This sweet bacon goes great with spicy meals.

THE VERY BEST BAKED APPLES

I love baked apples for breakfast and tend to fix them more if I don't try too hard to concoct fancy fillings. In other words, just bake the apples. Whenever I think of autumn in Santa Fe, I smell red chiles drying, cedar fires and apples because the apples grown in northern New Mexico are so very flavorful.

6 Golden Delicious apples (or your favorite baking apple)
6 teaspoons light brown sugar
6 heaping teaspoons frozen apple juice concentrate
  (undiluted)
1 cup frozen apple juice concentrate
1/2 cup water
6 teaspoons granulated sugar
1 and 1/2 teaspoons ground cinnamon

1. Remove cores of apples without going all the way to the bottoms of apples. Peel a strip around the top of each apple.

2. Place apples in a 9 by 13-inch baking dish. Place a teaspoon of brown sugar in each cored apple and then a heaping teaspoon of apple juice concentrate. In the dish place the rest of the concentrate and the water.

3. Cover the dish with foil. Bake in a preheated 375 degree F. oven for 45 minutes. Remove foil. Sprinkle the skins of each apple with a teaspoon of granulated sugar and some of the cinnamon. Bake the apples for 10 more minutes without covering.

4. Serve each apple with some of the marvelous juices from the pan or with some of Aunt Anna's Caramel Sauce or both. The apples keep well for a couple of days when refrigerated with the pan juices to keep them moist.

AUNT ANNA'S CARAMEL SAUCE

My husband's Aunt Anna operated an inn called Lindhome in southern Oregon during the 20's. She was a legendary cook who could make even the simplest things taste good and she always had a trick up her sleeve. This caramel sauce was one of them. Most often she used her sauce over cake, and then stale cake, and then over bread when she ran out of cake. The guests staying in Lindhome never knew what hit them because the The Caramel Sauce was so good. She always kept a jar of it to pull herself out of emergencies. It is divine served warm over simple baked apples like the ones above or try in over bread!

1 cup granulated sugar
1 tablespoon water
1/4 cup very hot water
1/2 cup whipping cream
2 tablespoons butter
1 teaspoon pure vanilla

1. Cook sugar and the 1 tablespoon water over low heat in heavy 2-quart saucepan until sugar dissolves. During the early stages of caramelization it is best to swirl the pan. Stirring during the first ten minutes encourages sugar to clump. When the bottom of saucepan is liquid caramel, then you can gently stir. After about 12 minutes, caramelization will be complete and you should have a golden syrup.

2. Remove from heat and at arm's length, add the 1/4 cup hot water. If you add it slowly it will not release as much steam. Cool the syrup for 5 minutes.

3. Next whisk in the cream and butter. Stir over low heat just until the syrup is smooth. Mixture will bubble. Remove caramel from heat and add the vanilla. Cool. Store in covered jar in refrigerator or serve immediately over baked apples, ice cream, cake, or cinnamon rolls. The caramel sauce will thicken when chilled but will thin out again when reheated gently. This recipe will make enough to serve over 8 cinnamon rolls, 8 pieces of cake, or 8 servings of ice cream (unless you eat too much out of the jar).

AUNT ANNA'S ORIGINAL RECIPE CALLED FOR THREE TIMES AS MUCH BUTTER MAKING A VERY THICK, BUTTERY CARAMEL.

BLUE CORN JALAPEÑO MUFFINS

Below is an adaptation of Chef Kip McClerin's recipe for Blue Corn Muffins, concocted when he was a chef at La Casa Sena in Santa Fe. The recipe eventually moved over to the Santa Fe School of Cooking where new touches were added so as to make use of the wonderful blue cornmeal that is specially ground for the market and cooking school. Now I have added my touches (less sugar and butter and more chiles).

1/2 cup softened butter
1/2 cup sugar
3 eggs
6 jalapeños, seeded and minced
1 cup corn kernels, fresh or canned
2 cups medium sharp Cheddar cheese, grated
1 cup all purpose flour
1 and 1/4 cups blue cornmeal
3 teaspoons baking powder
1 teaspoon salt

1. Preheat oven to 375 degrees F. Beat the softened butter until light and add sugar. Add 1 egg at a time to the mixture, beating well after each addition.

2. Add all the rest of the ingredients in the order given and stir just until blended. If batter seems runny, add 1/4 cup more all-purpose flour.

3. Spoon batter into greased 12-cup muffin tin. Bake for about 20 minutes or until golden.

LEFTOVER MUFFINS CAN BE CRUMBLED AND
MIXED WITH SAUTEED SAUSAGE, ONIONS, AND
CHOPPED APPLES TO MAKE A STUFFING FOR
CORNISH HENS OR CHICKENS.

BARBARA HUNTER'S SAGE WALNUT CORN CAKES

This recipe was given to me years ago by my friend Norma
who in turn obtained it from a talented cello musician
called Barbara. I am only sorry that I waited so long to
cook them as the corn cakes are fabulous with Southwestern foods. The marriage of the fresh sage and nuts is a
delicious one;enough so that the morning I made them, I
consumed one entire corn cake myself. No wonder it's
hard to be a skinny cookbook author.

1 cup milk
1 egg
5 tablespoons virgin olive oil
1 cup all purpose flour
1 cup finely ground cornmeal
2 tablespoons baking powder
2 tablespoons sugar
1 teaspoon salt
2/3 cup finely chopped walnuts (or pecans)
20 fresh sage leaves

  1. Combine milk, egg, and 3 tablespoons of the olive oil
and whisk together.

  2. Combine flour, cornmeal, baking powder, sugar, and
salt. Add the liquid mixture to the dry mixture and blend
well.

3. Heat 1 tablespoon olive oil in a nonstick, omelet pan (about 12 inches). When medium hot, sprinkle in half of the sage and half of the chopped nuts. Pour in half of the batter so that the corn cake is 1/2-inch thick. Cook until bottom of corn cake is golden brown and top is barely wet with bubbles appearing on the surface. Slide the cake onto a flat plate and then carefully invert back into the pan. Cook about 3 minutes longer.

4. Repeat the cooking procedure for the second corn cake. The flavor is so good the cakes need little more than a dab of butter or sour cream and they are good any time of day.

Makes 2 large 10-inch corn cakes to be cut into wedges for serving.

IT IS MOST IMPORTANT THAT YOU FIND FRESH SAGE IN THE MARKET OR YOUR OWN GARDEN.

TECOLOTE CAFE'S FAMOUS CINNAMON ROLLS

Bill and Alice Jennison, the owners and chefs of one of Santa Fe's most popular spots for breakfast say that there is practically a riot when they run out of these cinnamon rolls for the restaurant's breadbaskets. Because these do not require yeast, only baking powder, they can be assembled and baked in under an hour. Besides that they are one of the best cinnamon rolls I have ever tasted.

These are spirals of streusel layered in a baking powder biscuit dough.

2 cups all purpose flour
1 tablespoon sugar
4 teaspoons baking powder
1/2 teaspoon salt
1/2 teaspoon cream of tartar
1/2 cup shortening
3/4 cup milk

STREUSEL MIX

3 tablespoons melted butter
1 cup brown sugar
1 teaspoons cinnamon
1/2 cup pecans, finely chopped

1. Preheat oven to 400 degrees F. Toss together the flour, sugar, baking powder, salt, and cream of tartar.

2. Using a pastry blender or your fingertips, blend the shortening into the dry mixture until you have a bowl of fine crumbs.

3. Add ~~mix~~ milk to above mixture and stir with fork just until everything is moist. It is at this point that you do not want to overmix. Dump out the moistened dough onto a floured board. Use the heel of your hand to push into the dough and gently knead 10 times. Dough should be smooth.

4. If your bread board is now sticky, clean with a dough scraper. Sprinkle on more flour and push dough into a small rectangle and then use a rolling pin to achieve a larger rectangle about 1/4-inch thick. Brush on the melted butter, sprinkle with brown sugar, cinnamon, and nuts. Press the streusel mixture into the rectangle of dough so it doesn't pop out during baking.

5. Roll up the dough, starting from the long side, into a tight jelly roll. Slice off 1-inch thick cinnamon rolls. Place on baking sheet or jelly roll pan. Bake for about 15 minutes or until golden.

Makes 10 to 12 large cinnamon rolls.

HOTEL ST. FRANCIS CURRANT SCONES

These fragile scones served at the Hotel St. Francis in Santa Fe for their afternoon tea along with clotted cream and strawberry jam, make a nice breakfast. From the first time I tasted them, I knew I had to have the recipe and went in search of the person responsible for such delicate scones.

Missy McCoy, who was at the time the pastry chef at the St. Francis, received me in her kitchen at the hotel and graciously helped work out a home version of the recipe.

4 and 1/2 cups unbleached, all purpose flour
1/3 cup sugar
1 tablespoon plus 1 teaspoon baking powder
1 and 1/2 teaspoon salt
1 cup unsalted butter
3/4 to 1 cup currants
2 eggs
1 and 1/4 cups cream
1 egg beaten with 2 tablespoons milk
1/3 cup brown sugar for glaze

1. Preheat oven to 400 degrees F. Using a food processor, blend the flour, sugar, baking powder, and salt. Cut the butter into small pieces and add to the dry ingredients. Pulse until the butter and flour are blended and the mixture resembles cornmeal. Place the mixture in a large bowl and stir in the currants.

2. Beat eggs and cream together. Slowly drizzle 1/2 cup at a time over top and sides of dry ingredients, tossing the

mixture with a fork. Drizzle in the egg-cream mixture wherever the dough appears to be dry.

3. Loosely press the dough together and turn out onto a floured board. Knead 10 times to blend well. Discard any remaining dry crumbs. Roll out dough on a floured board until it is 1-inch thick. Cut into scones using 2-inch round cutter. Note that when you use the cutter, press it down into the dough to cut and then pull up. Do NOT twist the cutter or the scones won't rise properly. Place scones on baking sheet. If you place them several inches apart they will brown more.

4. Brush egg-milk wash over the top of each scone. Sieve brown sugar over the tops. Bake for 14 to 15 minutes, or until golden and the sugar has caramelized. Serve with clotted cream and jam or with lemon curd.

Makes 18 to 20 scones.

I JUST BAKE THE ODD PIECES OF DOUGH, RATHER THAN REROLL THE SCRAPS. MY FAMILY LOVES TO NIBBLE ON THESE ORPHAN SCONES.

SUSAN FRIEDER'S SUMMER FRUIT CRISP

If you are wondering why a fruit crisp is in a breakfast book, wonder no more. First of all, they are perfect for breakfast. Mitchell Frieder, the talented chef of Cakes and Company, makes it a practice to eat one of his wife's fruit crisps for breakfast whenever he can get away with it. The disgusting thing is that he looks like he has about 3 % body fat. The rest of us mortals are better off sharing an entire crisp and if you are serving a spicy Southwestern brunch, a fruit crisp makes a perfect ending. Or if you made a crisp the night before, sneak into the kitchen and have the leftovers for breakfast with cafe con leche.

Susan taught me that combining various fruits makes for even more delicious crisps or cobblers. In the recipe below, we blend sliced peaches, blueberries, and raspberries. Also wonderful are the combinations of peaches and strawberries or pears and raspberries.

The great attribute of Susan's crumb topping is that it doesn't sink into the fruit during baking but remains crumbly. Best of all, it is quite easy to put together especially if you have a food processor.

6 cups sliced fresh peaches, the sweetest you can find
1 cup fresh blueberries
1 cup fresh raspberries
3/4 cup to 1 cup sugar, depending upon sweetness of fruit
2 to 3 tablespoons cornstarch

CRISP TOPPING

2 and 1/2 cups all purpose flour
2 tablespoons granulated sugar
1 cup light brown sugar (well packed in cup)
6 ounces butter
1 and 1/2 cups finely minced pecans or walnuts
3/4 teaspoon cinnamon

1. Use a 2-inch deep 10-inch round baking dish or 9 x 13-inch baking pan or dish. It is important that you use something deep so the fruit doesn't bubble over the edges. Preheat oven to 400 degrees F.

2. Slice the peaches and stir in sugar and cornstarch, blending well. Gently add the berries.

3. Finely mince the nuts in a food processor or with a large knife. Set aside. Next combine the flour, sugar, brown sugar, cinnamon, and butter in the bowl of the food processor. Pulsate off and on until you have a crumb mixture. Stir in the minced nuts. This will give you approximately 6 cups crumb mixture or enough for 3 crisps. You will just need 2 cups crumbs for this peach berry crisp.

4. Sprinkle 2 cups of the crumb mixture over the fruit. If you want to bake a giant crisp for a large party, use a standard roasting pan, triple the amount of fruit, sugar, and cornstarch and use the total amount of crumb mixture on top. I usually just bake 1 fruit crisp with 2 cups crumbs (requiring 6 cups fruit as given in above recipe) and freeze the rest.

5. Bake the fruit crisp in the preheated oven for 15 minutes at 400 degrees F. Reduce temperature to 375 degrees F. and bake for approximately 15 minutes or until top is golden. For a larger crisp you will have to increase baking time by 20 to 30 minutes. Serve warm accompanied by softly whipped cream or just by itself.

Serves approximately 8 people or Susan's husband.

SUSAN ALWAYS KEEPS A PLASTIC CONTAINER
OF CRISP TOPPING IN THE FREEZER SO IF SHE
SUDDENLY NEEDS A DESSERT FOR UNEXPECTED
GUESTS, SHE JUST HAS TO SLICE FRUIT INTO A
BAKING DISH, MIX IN SUGAR AND CORNSTARCH,
SPRINKLE WITH TOPPING AND BAKE.
THE TOPPING KEEPS FOR MONTHS
IN THE FREEZER.

AHWAHNEE HOTEL CREAMED BANANAS

These bananas have been served at the Sunday brunch of the Ahwahnee Hotel in Yosemite for as long as anyone can remember and the recipe was given to me by Darlene, manager of the hotel dining room. Her first job there was mixing up Creamed Bananas seventeen years ago. Faithful hotel guests will not let them remove the bananas from the buffet. I frequently serve them with my spicy breakfasts and everyone always wants the recipe.

8 ounces cream cheese (reduced fat is also acceptable)
3 tablespoons whipping cream
2 tablespoons milk
1 teaspoon vanilla
1/4 teaspoon banana extract
1/8 teaspoon almond extract
5 ripe but not squishy bananas
1/2 cup fresh raspberries or 1/2 cup chopped pecans (in winter only)

1. Beat the cream cheese until softened and add the sugar. Whip several minutes until the sugar is dissolved. Add the cream, milk, and extracts to create a sauce consistency to easily coat the bananas.

2. Slice the bananas thickly right into the bowl of cream cheese mixture. Gently stir until all bananas are submerged. Place in refrigerator for at least an hour or two before serving. If the bananas are perfectly ripe they will give up some of their sweetness to the cream. Some people mistakenly think this is a rich banana pudding.

3. Spoon out small servings and sprinkle with fresh raspberries or chopped pecans.

Serves 6 to 8 as a side dish for brunch.

PECAN SOUR CREAM COFFEE CAKE

Santa Fe is a breakfast town which means that it is inescapably a baker's town. If you stay at a bed and breakfast inn you will probably be awakened by the aroma of biscuits, coffee cakes, and other sweet things enticing you to the table.

If you take a morning run around the plaza, you will pass the Plaza Bakery where people line up early for muffins. If you eat out in a restaurant, you may be offered homemade breads. Even if you tried, you couldn't escape all the baking. Counterbalancing all of the temptations is the fact that Santa Fe is also a walker's and runner's town besides being a baker's town. So we walk it off and then go back for more.

The first time we went to Santa Fe, we booked into the small, delightful bed and breakfast inn, Preston House, to celebrate our fifteenth wedding anniversary. By an amazing coincidence, the young woman who was running the inn and baking goodies for breakfast, was an acquaintance from San Miguel de Allende, Mexico where we had been married. We were treated like royalty by Christine and when we left she gave us the coffee cake recipe as a gift because we had loved it so.

2 sticks softened sweet butter (8 ounces)
1 and 1/2 cups sugar
2 eggs
1 cup sour cream
3 teaspoons pure vanilla
2 cups all-purpose flour
1/2 teaspoon salt
2 teaspoons baking powder
1 teaspoon baking soda

FILLING

4 tablespoons brown sugar
2 teaspoons cinnamon
1 cup chopped pecans
1/4 cup chopped dates or dried apricots
2 tablespoons softened butter

1. Preheat oven to 350 degrees F. Grease a 1 and 1/2 quart tube or bundt pan. For the filling, mix together the brown sugar, cinnamon, nuts, dates, and butter until crumbly. Set aside until you have completed the batter. Beat the butter and sugar together with an electric mixer until light. Add eggs, one at a time, and beat for another 2 minutes. Stir in sour cream and vanilla.

2. In a separate bowl stir together the flour, salt, baking powder, and baking soda until well-combined. Then add the dry mixture to the butter mixture, stirring just until blended. Do not overmix.

3. Pour half of the batter into the prepared pan. Sprinkle in the filling and then cover with the rest of the coffee cake batter. Bake for 1 hour. Cool at least 20 min-

utes before slicing. The cake is rich and resembles more of a pound cake than a traditional coffee cake.

Serves 8 to 10.

CHRISTINE VARIED THE FILLING, ADDING WHAT-
EVER SHE HAD ON HAND. SOMETIMES SHE USED
CHOCOLATE CHIPS AND NUTS OR GRATED
CHOCOLATE AND MINCED, DRIED FIGS.

PEAR BREAD

I like this quick bread far better than the ubiquitous banana bread. The chunks of pear are a delight and everyone is happy to eat something different. Slices beautifully, keeps well, and is good on your own bed and breakfast table.

1/2 cup softened sweet butter
1 cup sugar
2 large eggs
2 cups all-purpose flour
1/2 teaspoon salt
1/2 teaspoon baking soda
1 teaspoon baking powder
1/8 teaspoon or a pinch ground nutmeg
1/4 cup buttermilk
2 teaspoons pure vanilla
1 and 1/2 cups chopped pears
1/2 cup chopped nuts (pecans or walnuts)

1. Preheat oven to 350 degrees F. Grease a 8 x 4 -inch loaf pan. Beat the butter and sugar together until light. Add eggs 1 at a time, beating well after each addition.

2. Combine the dry ingredients and add to the butter-sugar mixture alternating with the buttermilk. Add vanilla.

3. Add pears and nuts. Bake at 350 degrees F. for 1 hour.

Makes 1 loaf of Pear Bread.

FOR SPECIAL OCCASIONS I HAVE MADE A GLAZE
OF SIEVED APRICOT JAM THINNED WITH A
TABLESPOON OF GRAND MARNIER. BRUSH ONTO
THE TOP OF STILL WARM PEAR BREAD.

CAPIROTADA

Capirotada is the bread pudding of the Southwest and it
would be remiss not to include it here because some people
love it for breakfast. What makes it really good is to include little surprises. If you have dry cinnamon rolls or a
couple of pieces of the pear bread above, include it in the
pudding with the day-old French bread.

This is a dish for cholesterol watchers because capirotada
has no eggs or milk and you can pare down the amount of
butter and cheese used. Reduce the butter to 1 tablespoon
and use reduced-fat cream cheese if you are watching your
diet and still want something sweet.

12 slices French bread or interesting combination
  of breads, torn into pieces
1 and 1/2 cups sugar
1 and 1/2 cups water
1 cup apple juice
3 tablespoons butter
1/2 cup raisins
1/2 cup piñon nuts or chopped pecans
1 teaspoon cinnamon
2 teaspoons vanilla extract
1/2 cup shredded Monterey Jack or Longhorn cheese
1 3-ounce package cream cheese, in small pieces

1. Preheat oven to 350 degrees F. and butter a deep 9 x 13-inch baking dish. Add the torn pieces of bread. Toast in oven for 10 minutes.

2. Meanwhile, over medium high heat stir sugar continuously in a saucepan until it melts and turns a light caramel color. Immediately add water and apple juice. Be careful; the caramel will bubble and splatter. The caramel will partially solidify but will liquefy again as you heat it. Add butter and raisins. When caramel is completely liquefied, remove from heat and stir in vanilla.

3. Pour caramel over bread pieces in the baking dish. Make sure bread is well soaked with caramel. Sprinkle top with piñon nuts or pecans, cinnamon, and cheeses. The cheese is a very Mexican and Southwestern touch (they usually add more!) and if you think you won't like it, just try a little because the taste of sweet caramel and the slight saltiness of the cheese is very delicious. Serve while warm with whipped cream.

Makes 8 servings of pudding.

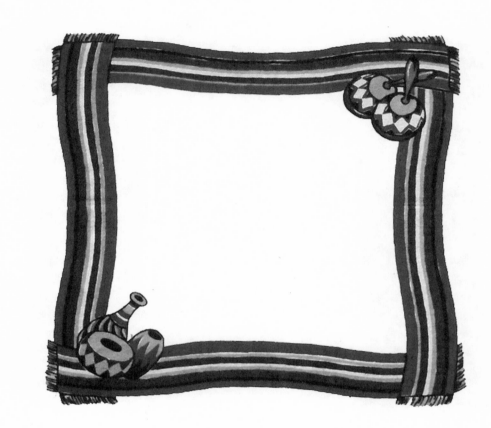

CHAPTER III

BREAKFAST ON A RANCHO

In the olden days, before civilization overtook California, missions were a day's horseback ride apart. Ranchos were separated by a couple of hours. There were no hotels for travelers who were often dependent upon the hospitality of the rancho. A guest was welcomed to a place at the family table with plenty to eat and a bed even if it was a straw mat in the bodega. You weren't even asked how long you planned to stay.

Rancho cooking was historically abundant. If you spent all day on horseback as did the rancheros and vaqueros or much of your day outdoors, you most naturally began with a robust breakfast or desayuno, the sort of all-inclusive breakfast that others might call a dinner.

It is only within the last fifty years that a narrow idea of breakfast food developed, the idea that only cereal, pancakes or waffles, and eggs were appropriate in the morning. A ludicrous concept to cowboys or vaqueros, farmers, or loggers. Breakfast was a meal that often had to sustain one all day. They wanted meat and some very solid starch in the form of potatoes, frijoles, tortillas, or biscuits and they wanted them to line the table in the style of a groaning board. The day was meant to be started with a gargantuan meal. There's probably a few people around who still subscribe to the theory that breakfast should be fit for a king or at least a cowboy.

On the Spanish ranchos of California, the customary foods eaten bore quite a resemblance to those preferred by the Southwestern Spaniards, cousins in the grand scheme of eating. This is not surprising for they shared a heritage from Spain and Mexico. All foreigners, a term loosely applied to Anglos particularly those mild souls from Boston, looked askance at what was consumed for breakfast. The opinion was widely held that the Spaniards had the digestion of ostriches considering the fact that they gladly ate red chile anytime of the day and especially for breakfast!

CHORIZO

One of the great discoveries made by early Southwestern and rancho cooks was the preservation of meats with red chile which serves as an antioxidant. Carne seca or beef jerky was made by dipping strips of meat into chile puree and then hanging it out to dry. By mixing ground meats with potent red chile and vinegar, sausages can be kept for days without using preservatives like nitrates. Thus chorizo, one of the best loved sausages on ranchos and in the Southwest, was invented.

It is difficult to buy good chorizo. Sometimes the stuff in the tubes has so much fat and unmentionables, it hard to find the actual sausage in proportion to fat once it is cooked. One of my fondest memories of childhood snacks are chorizo and egg sandwiches on white bread. My mother wrapped these spicy sandwiches in paper towels and handed them out the backdoor. The neighborhood kids used to beg us to trade them for their baloney ones. Not a chance.

2 pounds unseasoned ground pork (not sausage)
1 pound ground turkey
1 tablespoon finely minced garlic
2 to 3 tablespoons dried oregano
1 and 1/2 teaspoons black pepper
1 heaping tablespoon crushed cumin seed
1 tablespoon kosher salt
1/2 teaspoon canela (Mexican cinnamon)
4 tablespoons ground California chile, pasilla, or ancho

4 tablespoons New Mexican ground red chile
2 to 4 tablespoons New Mexican chile caribe (crushed
chile with seeds)
1/2 cup apple cider vinegar, warmed

1. First marinate the chile caribe and 2 tablespoons ground New Mexican chile in the warm vinegar for 30 minutes to create a paste.

2. Place the ground pork and turkey into a bowl and mix in all the rest of the ingredients including the chile paste. You may use all ground pork if you like.

3. Let the flavors of the chorizo marinate for at least an hour before you use it. Freeze any leftover chorizo in 1/2 pound portions in zip-loc plastic bags. It will keep for several months when frozen and is great to add to beans, paella, tinga, or for chorizo and eggs.

Makes 3 pounds chorizo.

CHORIZO AND EGGS

1/2 pound chorizo
6 to 8 eggs, beaten

1. Fry chorizo in a nonstick skillet over medium low heat for 10 minutes. Remove pan from heat and push chorizo to one side. Wipe up any excess grease with paper towels. Put pan back over medium heat and add the eggs. Cook until eggs are set and well mixed with chorizo.

2. Serve chorizo and eggs as is or in soft tacos or make sandwiches. Above amount will make 4 to 6 sandwiches. Serve with pickled jalapeños for garnish.

CHORIZO TOSTADA

Rancho cooks always had flour tortillas on hand. If they are a day old and a little dry, they are good for tostadas. As a little girl cook, I used to place a flour tortilla directly over the gas flame of my mother's stove, lay slices of Cheddar cheese over the tortilla and then stand and watch the cheese melt. The tortilla would become golden crisp and maybe a little burnt on the bottom. Smelling the burning tortilla all the way out to the garden where she spent much of her time, Mama came running into the kitchen and I was scolded about my dangerous cooking habits.

This scenario was repeated many times over and if she was still here, she would probably scold me about my dangerous cooking (especially if she saw me blackening chiles with a blow torch).

An easier method is using the oven for crisping flour tortillas.

1 pound cooked and drained chorizo
4 small flour tortillas (7-inches)
3 teaspoons oil
2 cups grated Cheddar cheese
4 eggs
Mike's Hot Chile Sauce

1. Preheat oven to 500 degrees. Oil 2 baking sheets in readiness for the tostadas. Fill a bowl with water and dip one tortilla at a time quickly into water and then place 2 on each baking sheet. Bake in oven for approximately 3 minutes or until tortillas turn a golden color. Reduce oven heat to 375 degrees F.

2. Remove baking sheets from oven and poke any puffed spots on the tortillas. Crumple chorizo and cheese in a round border circling each tortilla, covering the edges but leaving the center for the egg. Break an egg into the center of each tortilla. Bake the tostadas at 375 degrees F. for about 5 minutes. The whites should be set but you must determine if the yolks are cooked to your preference.

3. Place a tostada on each plate. Pass Mike's Hot Chile Sauce to drizzle on eggs. You can accompany these with refried beans.

Serves 4.

MIKE'S HOT CHILE SAUCE

Mike is the Michael Sherrell who is the publisher of *The Californians* , an excellent history publication, and apparently the only bone he has to pick with me is that my chile sauce recipe isn't hot enough. He prefers to leave in the chile seeds. Little does he know that when I make my chile sauce (seeds or no seeds) with certain New Mexican chiles, it is HOT ENOUGH for chile aficionados.

Because all chiles are so unpredictable, you might use a certain kind of chile for your sauce and find it too mild. The next time you use the same chile type, the sauce is too hot. The one thing that is predictable about chiles is that they are mostly unpredictable.

Mike's version of chile sauce is very flavorful and I especially like all the garlic.

6 large dried red chile pods (California or New Mexican)
Water to cover
3 to 4 tablespoons minced garlic
1/2 cup minced onion
1/2 teaspoon salt
1/3 cup cider vinegar
Fresh water to cover
Another couple cloves of minced garlic just for
  good measure

   1. Rinse the dust and grit off the chile pods. Break off stems but do not discard seeds. Place chiles in pot and just cover with water, probably about 4 cups.

2. Add garlic, onion, salt, and vinegar. Simmer the chiles partially covered for about 45 minutes or until liquid is almost gone. Drain off excess liquid.

3. Place chile mixture in food processor or blender, adding from 1/2 cup to 1 cup fresh water. Just barely cover the chiles. Puree. Add more garlic if desired. Mike says, "Put in an innocent-looking glass jar, close tightly and label prominently."

Makes about 1 and 1/2 cups.

RED ENCHILADAS

When breakfast was served on the California ranchos, it often included leftovers from the day before. Just as in the Southwest, frijoles and tortillas were always included. No one could imagine a table without beans. In addition to fried or scrambled eggs, it was considered a treat to have leftover tamales, empanadas, fruit pies, and red enchiladas. A sizzled fried egg perched on top of a warmed over red enchilada makes one of the best breakfasts I know.

Whenever I make these enchiladas, my husband cautions me to reserve a couple for breakfast. I got in trouble one year at a family reunion when I dutifully hid a pan of particularly succulent red enchiladas, made by one of the best cooks, for breakfast the next day. The irate cook saw me spirit them away and told my mother-in-law who told me not to steal enchiladas. The next morning she joined us for red enchiladas.

In my *California Rancho Cooking*, I give a recipe for the traditional red chile sauce which is the basis for so many recipes in California and the Southwest. Below, is a quicker version. In our family when you referred to using Las Palmas, you meant the canned red chile puree which, even years ago, was considered a good, respectable substitute for homemade.

My mother and grandmother, who were great cooks, often relied on Las Palmas in a pinch. I find canned red chile thinner these days so I just soak a couple of red chiles for 20 minutes in hot water and then puree the chiles and spices with Las Palmas. The trick is to use very good dried red chiles that will add to the flavor.

QUICK RED CHILE SAUCE

2 dried California or New Mexican chiles
Boiling water to cover
1/2 cup chicken stock
1 large can Las Palmas red chile sauce
  (or other good brand)
1 teaspoon oregano
2 cloves minced garlic
1 tablespoon cider vinegar

1. Rinse dust and grit off chiles. Remove stems and seeds. Place in bowl and cover with boiling water. Allow the chiles to steep until puffed and softened, about 20 minutes. Drain off water.

2. Place chiles in food processor or blender, adding the stock, half of the canned sauce, the oregano, garlic, and vinegar. Puree until everything is well-blended. Pour into saucepan, adding the rest of the canned chile sauce. Simmer for 20 minutes so flavors come together and sauce reduces a little.   Set aside while you prepare the rest of the ingredients.

ASSEMBLING ENCHILADAS:

8 10-inch fresh flour tortillas (do not use corn tortillas)
3 tablespoons olive oil
5 medium onions, finely chopped
1 and 1/2 pounds medium sharp Cheddar cheese
1 large can pitted black olives
2 tablespoons olive oil for frying eggs
1 egg to top each enchilada

124

1. Heat oil in large skillet and very slowly sauté onions for 25 to 30 minutes. The onions will reduce to an onion marmalade, becoming sweet and succulent. This is the most crucial step to the recipe.

2. Arrange the flour tortillas, warm red chile sauce, grated cheese, and olives in your enchilada assembly line. Use a wide, flat dinner plate for filling the dipped tortillas. Have 2 long, greased baking pans ready for enchiladas. Begin your assembly.

3. Dip a flour tortilla on both sides in the red chile sauce until it is completely masked. Lay on the plate. Down the center of the dipped tortilla place about 1/4 cup grated cheese, 1/4 cup sautéed onions, and 2 olives. Fold over the sides and gently lift the huge enchilada , seam down, into a long, greased pan. You can assemble these the day before you need them. They will just gain flavor as the chile penetrates the tortilla. Sprinkle a few tablespoons of sauce over the tops of the enchiladas just before heating in a 350 degree oven.

4. Bake enchiladas in the preheated oven for about 20 minutes or until cheese is melted and enchiladas are puffed. Do not overbake as the edges of the enchiladas will dry out. Only bake as many enchiladas as you plan to serve. Or just make them all one day and serve them all to a lucky group of people for breakfast, brunch, or supper the next day. While the breakfast enchiladas are baking, fry enough eggs to place on each hot enchilada. Accompany with refried beans, tortillas, fruit, and cafe con leche.

Makes 8 huge enchiladas.

IF YOU ARE ON A LOW FAT DIET, FILL THE ENCHI-
LADAS WITH LESS CHEESE AND USE A CHEESE
WITH REDUCED FAT. SAUTE ONIONS IN A
NONSTICK PAN WITH 1 TEASPOON OLIVE OIL.

FLOUR TORTILLAS OF THE RANCHO

The perfection of one's flour tortillas was the gauge by
which a rancho cook was judged. One family insisted on
crepelike, thin tortillas and another family liked them thick
and chewy. It is all a matter of personal preference but in
our family, we valued the delicate tortilla, rolled thin and
then handstretched.

Rolling and handstretching tortillas is as therapeutic as
kneading bread. Somewhere I nurture a hope that making
flour tortillas by hand will not become a lost art. The taste is
incomparable and if you have homemade flour tortillas you
can make some of the best enchiladas you'll ever taste.

I have bowed to health concerns and changed my mother's
and grandmother's traditional recipe by replacing the shortening with canola oil. I am indebted to the test cooks of the
Eating Well magazine for discovering the trick of freezing
part of the flour and oil so that the mixture simulates vegetable shortening. This results in flour tortillas so flaky you
would think that they were the traditional ones. They also
puff on the griddle, something that storebought tortillas
almost never do.

4 cups all-purpose flour
1 and 1/2 teaspoons salt
1/2 teaspoon baking powder
4 tablespoons canola oil
1 and 1/2 cups warm water

1. Sift flour and baking powder together. Remove 1/2 cup of flour mixture and use a fork to blend the canola oil into this flour. When well-blended, place in a plastic bag and freeze for an hour.

2. Use a fork to blend the cold flour-oil mixture into the dry flour mixture until it resembles pastry crumbs. Mix the salt into the warm water and drizzle into the flour mixture until you can make a soft ball of dough. Knead the dough for 1 minute in the bowl. Cover with plastic wrap and let it rest for 30 minutes to 2 hours at room temperature.

3. Oil a jelly roll pan and then form the dough into 14 balls. Flatten balls into 3-inch discs and allow them to rest for 30 minutes, covered in plastic wrap so they don't dry out. The 2 rests not only help the dough mellow but also relax so it is much easier to work with.

4. Preheat a griddle or comal. Dust a floured board and place a flattened tortilla ball in center. Roll dough into a circle, rolling from center out. Make a quarter turn of the tortilla after each 2 strokes so your tortilla will remain round. The perfect tool for rolling is a sawed-off, clean broom handle or 7-inch piece of wooden dowel.

5. After you have rolled the tortilla to an 8-inch circle, handstretch it to a 10-inch circle. Hang tortilla from the fingertips of one hand (if you are right-handed, drape tortilla

from your left hand or vice versa) and draw the fingers of the opposing hand underneath tortilla. The fingers should pull and stretch in a gentle fashion. Do this a couple of times in each direction under the tortilla as you hold it. You will have a delicately thin tortilla that cannot be achieved by rolling on a board just as pizza makers finish off their pizza by tossing it in the air. When I am frustrated with something, stretching tortillas like this restores my universe.

6. Place tortilla on heated comal with medium flame under it. Keep turning tortilla every 10 seconds. It will get light brown freckles and puff in spots. Do not push on the tortilla when it is puffing as this is just the formation of delicate layers. You will have to turn it 4 or 5 times on the comal. When the tortilla stops puffing, it is done. The homemade flour tortilla cooks in less than a minute. If you overcook them they will become very dry. Place the cooked tortillas inside a tea towel. Do not place in plastic or they will sweat.

Makes 12 to 14 tortillas. Eat them as is or use for breakfast burritos or Red Enchiladas.

FRIJOLES

The entire cuisine of the ranchos was based on red chiles and beans. Since there were always leftover beans, they naturally became refried the next day. When I tried to recreate Grandma's beans from memory I failed miserably until I learned patience with the second simmering of the beans. It's all in the rhythm of the simmering and the mashing.

FIRST COOK THE BEANS:

1 pound pink beans or pintos
1 chopped onion
2 cloves minced garlic
2 teaspoons New Mexican chile powder
2 teaspoons salt or salt to your taste

1. Rinse beans in sieve and pick over for stones. Cover beans with water, bring to boil, and simmer 3 minutes. Let beans soak for at least 2 to 4 hours. Pour off this soaking liquid.

2. Cover beans with 6 cups of fresh water, onion, garlic, and chile powder. Simmer for about 2 hours or until tender but not mushy. The presoaked beans may also be cooked for 50 minutes in a pressure cooker.

THE ART OF THICK BEANS:

1 tablespoon canola oil or mild olive oil
1/2 teaspoon fine pepper
All of the above beans with 1 and 1/2 cups
  reserved bean liquor

1. Heat the oil in a cast- iron pan. Add pepper, 1/2 cup beans and 1/4 cup bean liquor. When mixture bubbles, mash beans with back of large spoon or even better a bean masher. Leave some beans whole.

2. When beans in pan are thickened, add another 1/2 cup beans and some bean liquor. Do not add too much of liquid at any one time. Keep up the zen balance of thickening and adding beans and bean liquor. It is all gradual but takes no more than 20 minutes. Hold back on adding all of the bean liquor if the beans are as thick as you want them. They also thicken quite a bit upon refrigeration. Serves 6 to 8 as a side dish.

Traditionally, Mexican cooks add about 1/2 cup melted lard to the beans to make them creamy. This method does make the beans creamy but eventually delivers you to the cardiac ward especially if you eat beans everyday. By using a scant amount of oil and using the bean liquor to create the creaminess, you will eat a lot healthier.

REFRIED BEANS OR REFRITOS

2 tablespoons canola or olive oil
2 cups cold thick beans (from above recipe)
2 tablespoons grated Parmesan cheese

1. Heat the oil in a cast-iron skillet and add beans all at once. Press into a large pancake. Cook until the edges are sizzled and starting to crisp around the edges. Sprinkle with cheese and serve.

Serves 4.

TORTILLA ESPAÑOLA-SPANISH OMELET

When the Spanish soldados de cuera (leather-jacketed soldiers) took the overland route to settle the outpost of Alta California, they brought with them Spanish food customs blended with those that they had adopted from the Mexican Indians.

In Spain an omelet is called a tortilla. When the soldados and conquistadores saw the Mexicans cooking flat corn cakes, they named them tortillas like their Spanish omelets.

The Tortilla Española is one of the most savory egg dishes I know and because it tastes wonderful just at room temperature it is perfect for late brunches and picnics. This dish was one of my grandmother's standbys. She always kept a couple of cooked potatoes in the icebox and always used good olives, homemade or Spanish. The olives finish off the omelet to perfection.

2 Russet potatoes
2 tablespoons olive oil
1/2 cup chopped red onion
1 red bell pepper or 1 cup roasted red pepper from jar
8 eggs, beaten
2 tablespoons grated Parmesan cheese
1/4 cup black Spanish olives
  or Kalamata olives, pitted, sliced
1 tablespoon minced parsley

1. Cook the potatoes in water to cover just until tender. This will take about 25 minutes. Cool until easy to handle. Slice very thin.

2. Heat olive oil in a 12-inch nonstick skillet. Sauté onion. When softened push to one side of skillet and saute the potatoes slices until golden.

3. Meanwhile, broil or roast the red pepper until skin is blistered. Remove skin. If you are in a hurry substitute the roasted red peppers found in jars. Cut pepper into strips, reserving a few for garnish. Add 3/4 cup peppers to the potatoes in skillet. Pour beaten eggs over the top. Turn heat to low.

4. Shake the pan and tilt so that the uncooked eggs run to the edges and bottom. The omelet will take from 4 to 5 minutes to cook. In Spain, the cook slides the omelet onto a flat plate after first loosening around the edges and then flips the omelet upside down back into the pan so as to finish cooking. Easier but less dramatic is to place the omelet 8 inches under a broiler. The runny egg on top of omelet will quickly cook.

5. Before top of omelet is completely set, garnish with the remaining strips of red pepper, olives, and grated cheese. Slide under preheated broiler again and cook for about a minute. It doesn't take long.

6. Just before serving sprinkle the omelet with parsley. Cut into wedges. In Spain, the Tortilla Española is eaten at room temperature for brunch, picnics, and as a snack at tapas bars.

Serves 6.

UNCLE JACK'S MENUDO, THE BREAKFAST OF CHAMPIONS

There is such a cult among Spanish-speaking people concerning menudo recipes that it all boils down to one thing. Everyone makes the best menudo. Everyone's mother made the best menudo.

Arguments about the right way to cook menudo are ad infinitum. One of my remaining Spanish uncles, Uncle Jack, is a discriminating cook in his own right and now proudly wears the mantle of being the family's best menudo cook. Unless you ask the opinion of his otherwise loving yet disrespectful son. He thinks he cooks menudo better than his father.

There is no answer except to join in the fray and make your own.

The main ingredient of the "breakfast of champions" is honeycomb tripe which is the delicate stomach lining of the cow. Uncle Jack's directions can be found in no other menudo recipe. His secret is to remove every bit of fat from the tripe, to rinse it well, and to precook it separately. Ultimately, you'll have a broth of incomparable flavor.

1 veal knuckle
1 to 2 pounds neck bones
2 large cans of beef stock
Water to cover
1 tablespoon garlic
1 teaspoon salt
4 pounds honeycomb tripe (trepa)
Water to cover

2 cups chopped onions
1/2 cup ground red chile
2 whole dried California chiles
1/4 cup tablespoons minced cilantro
2 cloves minced garlic
3 teapoons cumin seed
1 tablespoon oregano blossoms or dried oregano
2 teaspoons salt
1 large can white hominy, drained

1. You'll need 2 separate large pots. Put the veal knuckle and neck bones in 1 pot. Cover with beef stock and water. Bring to a boil and turn down heat to low. Keep skimming off foam until water remains clear. Then stir in the salt and minced garlic.

2. Rinse the tripe extremely well in running water and cut off any visible fat and discard. Cut tripe into bite-sized pieces. Place in the second pot, cover with water, and gently simmer separately for 1 hour. DO NOT BOIL as this will toughen the tripe. Then place in a colander and rinse off in hot tap water. Now the tripe is ready to add to the stock.

3. Add tripe to the pot of beef stock along with chopped onions, the chile powder, and the whole chiles. Using a mortar and pestle (or small grinder) mash the cilantro, garlic, salt, cumin, and oregano into a paste. Stir it into the pot. Simmer the menudo for about 5 hours. If you plan on using fresh nixtamal you should add it here. It needs to cook several hours. If you are using canned hominy add it during the last hour of cooking. Again, do not allow the menudo to boil as it will make the tripe tough.

4. To further degrease the menudo before serving you can chill it over night in the refrigerator and skim off any fat that rises to the surface. You can pass lime wedges, chopped cilantro, and chopped green onions to be added as condiments to the bowls of menudo but many menudo fanciers consider this only so much fluff and require only the real thing-just a pure bowl of menudo.

Serves about 10 people.

FOR MORE FLAVOR PURCHASE FRESH NIXTAMAL FROM A MEXICAN GROCERY STORE. NIXTAMAL WHICH IS FRESH HOMINY IS SOAKED IN LIME SO NEEDS TO BE RINSED SEVERAL TIMES IN RUNNING WATER. AFTER THE BEEF STOCK HAS BEEN SKIMMED ADD THE NIXTAMAL AND COOK FOR SEVERAL HOURS UNTIL TENDER. ADD 3 CUPS NIXTAMAL IN PLACE OF THE CANNED HOMINY.

HANGTOWN FRY

In the West this was the most famous breakfast dish. No one knows for sure if the concoction was really invented in Placerville, formerly Hangtown, as was loudly proclaimed but San Francisco took Hangtown Fry to its heart. The old Palace Hotel became famous for it. A lot of cooks claimed that they invented it.

When goldminers poured into The City with their newfound wealth, one of the first things they wanted, other than a new suit of clothes, was fresh oysters, eggs, and champagne.

All cooks faithfully follow a standard of dusting the fresh oysters with seasoned flour, dipping them in beaten egg, and then rolling in cracker crumbs (you can also use fresh breadcrumbs).

12 small oysters
1/2 cup flour
1 teaspoon salt
1/2 teaspoon pepper
1/2 teaspoon paprika
1/4 teaspoon cayenne pepper
2 eggs for dipping
2 cups finely crushed saltine crackers
1/2 cup canola oil for frying oysters
2 tablespoons butter
8 eggs for omelet, beaten
4 strips of crisply fried bacon

1. Pat oysters dry and roll in mixture of flour, salt, pepper, paprika, and cayenne pepper.

2. Dip oysters in beaten egg and then roll in cracker crumbs until well-coated.

3. Heat oil in nonstick skillet and sauté oysters, in batches, until golden brown on both sides. Drain most of the oil from skillet and add the butter. When butter is hot, return all the fried oysters to the pan and pour in the eggs. Lift up the cooked edges of egg, allowing liquid portion to flow to edges, much as you do with an omelet. Cook slowly until egg is set. Serve with bacon crumbled over the top.

Serves 4.

NOPAL (CACTUS) OMELET

Nopales or cactus pads have long been a delicacy appreci-
ated in California, parts of the Southwest, and Mexico.
They were part of the wild food, along with verdolagas,
purslane, mushrooms, and mustard greens which brought
some green stuff into a diet which consisted largely of meat,
frijoles, tortillas, and dried chiles.

Most of the ranchos grew cactus as part of the fencing sur-
rounding the family's abode. The variety most often used
was the Opuntia, or prickly pear cactus. Cactus pads in
their prime should be bright green and, when young, look
like fingers attached to a big hand.

2 small nopales
1 tablespoon olive oil
1/2 diced red bell pepper
1/2 cup diced red onion
1 jalapeño chile, seeded and minced
2 tablespoons minced cilantro
2 cups grated Monterey Jack cheese
2 tablespoons butter
10 eggs for 4 omelets

1. To clean each nopal or cactus pad of any spines, hold
with tongs as you lay it on paper towels. Use a sharp little
knife to cut off each node, the base of each spine. Do not try
to hold cactus with your fingers or you may end up with
spines in your hand. Peel around the top edge of paddle,
where nodes are closer together. Trim off blunt end where

paddle was cut from the plant. You do not have to peel off the outer skin as some directions might advise. The old time cactus cooks are against this practice because it makes the entire pad release too much juice. As you peel the cactus, it will weep a little sticky juice. Just wipe it up with paper towels and clean your knife.

2. Bring 3 quarts water to boil and blanch the cactus pads for 1 minute. Drain immediately in colander under cold running water. The key is to rinse well. Cut the cactus into narrow strips about the width of a green bean and then dice the strips. Rinse the diced cactus again in the colander under cold running water.

3. Sauté the red pepper and onion in the olive oil just until slightly softened. Add the diced nopales, jalapeño, and cilantro and sauté a minute longer. This will be your omelette filling along with the grated cheese.

4. Beat the eggs just until blended. Heat 1/2 tablespoon butter in a 10 to 12- inch nonstick skillet. When butter is bubbling add just enough egg to coat the bottom of skillet. Swirl pan and lift cooked edges of egg to allow runny portion to flow underneath. When omelet is almost set, add about 1/3 cup grated cheese and about 1/3 cup of cactus filling. Fold sides of omelette inward and tip onto a warm plate. Garnish with a little of the filling and salsa.

Makes 4 omelets.

LOOK FOR NOPALES WITH BRIGHT GREEN SKIN, PADDLES WITH AN ELONGATED SHAPE, AND NO SHRIVELING.

PEACH PIE FOR BREAKFAST

Anyone who has been around logging camp cookhouses, California ranchos, Texas ranches, or truckdriver cafes knows that leftover pie for breakfast is not only acceptable but expected. If the cook made pie for dinner, it is only normal to put all leftover pie on the breakfast table.

The technique given below for making pie crust is that of my mother, a legendary pie maker, who learned the art from her blind Aunt Nick who resided on the family's land grant rancho in Milpitas, California.

Mama never bothered with chilled shortening although she always kept a glass of water filled with ice cubes to dip into while making pies. As children we loved to drink the ice water and make her yell. She never chilled her dough before rolling, probably because on the rancho the old ice box wouldn't chill it enough to make a difference. Her pie crust was very fragile and she always said that a piece of pie wasn't any good if it didn't fall apart when you tried to serve it.

2 cups all purpose flour
1/2 teaspoon salt
2/3 cup Crisco
1 tablespoon lemon juice
1 egg
2 and 1/2 tablespoons ice water
5 cups sliced peaches
1 cup sugar
1 tablespoon lemon juice
3 tablespoons cornstarch

1. Preheat oven to 375 degrees. In bowl, slice the peaches and add sugar, lemon juice, and cornstarch. Set aside while you make the pastry. Blend flour and salt together. Cut shortening in with a fork and finish blending with your fingertips until mixture is like breadcrumbs.

2. Beat lemon juice, egg, and ice water together. Drizzle into dry ingredients using fork to lift and blend. Form lightly and quickly into mound of dough. Divide dough in half for top and bottom crusts. Use light motion with rolling pin, rolling from center outward. Place bottom crust in 9-inch pie dish.

3. Fill with peaches. Roll out top crust and place on top of fruit. Pinch top and bottom crusts together using forefinger to form a little fluted edge around pie. Cut a vent in the top crust to release steam.

4. Sprinkle with sugar and bake pie for about 45 minutes or until crust is golden.

NORMA'S APRICOT JAM

According to Norma, do not bother making this jam if your apricots are not fragrant and do not have a flowery "nose".

One of the wonderful things about spending the night out at Norma's ranch in San Luis Obispo, is the anticipation of an enchanting breakfast. The tiny breakfast table for two sits against a large window facing her garden. Norma gets up early and bustles around the kitchen making biscuits and squeezing oranges on a funny little plastic squeezer. The orange juice is poured into wine goblets.

The table has an array of jellies and jams laid out like brightly colored jewels The apricot is my favorite. Coffee is poured into French Haviland cups, white and thin as egg-shells. They are among her most prized possessions and she always takes them out of seclusion for my visits because she knows that I love them so. Anything tastes better in these cups.

THIS JAM IS PARTICULARLY GOOD BECAUSE IT RELIES ONLY ON THE NATURAL PECTIN OF THE APRICOTS. IT IS A RECIPE FOR PEOPLE WHO LIKE SOFT JAM AS OPPOSED TO HEAVY JAM.

3 cups apricots
2 and 1/4 cup sugar
2 tablespoons lemon or lime juice

1. Cut up apricots into small pieces. Put into a large glass or ceramic bowl. Add sugar and juice and allow to marinate for 1 hour.

2. Place sugared fruit and juices in a large heavy pot over medium heat. It will take about 10 minutes to come to a boil. Then boil for 1 minute. Skim off foam. From the time that the jam boils, cook for another 10 minutes. Place a spoon of jam on a small plate so you can see the consistency. It should be buttery according to Norma.

3. Remove from heat and pour into sterile jars. Seal with sterilized lids.

AUDREY'S LEMON CURD

Because of the great influx out West of English settlers, certain charming customs such as afternoon tea were quickly adopted by the Spanish settlers who had no problem with tortillas for breakfast and lunch and scones for tea. Many of the ranchos in California served merienda, their version of afternoon tea.

One of the most delicious afternoon teas, that I never miss when in Santa Fe, is that served at the St. Francis Hotel. Ladies in stunning turquoise jewelry and denim and gentlemen in dress Stetsons recline in antique easy chairs, completely at ease with cucumber sandwiches and scones with Devonshire cream, strawberry jam, and lemon curd.

My step-mother, Audrey, mastered her Lemon Curd to such a degree that she sold it to gourmet shops in Palo Alto. Audrey's Lemon Curd on scones, biscuits, or golden toast is one of my favorites for breakfast and tea. It has a rich, smooth flavor but calls for less butter than most curd recipes.

3 cups sugar
1/4 pound sweet butter
4 eggs
A few grains of salt
Grated rind of 2 lemons
Juice of 4 lemons or enough
  to make 2/3 cup juice

1. In top of double boiler over simmering water, melt the butter. Add well-beaten eggs, salt, rind, lemon juice, and sugar.

2. Cook slowly, stirring occasionally until it is thick enough to spread. This will take about 45 minutes. Place in sterilized jars and when cool place in refrigerator.

Makes about 2 pints.

PALILLAS

No collection of Rancho or Southwestern breakfasts would be complete without Palillas. These pastries, prepared as a great delicacy by rancho cooks, are cousins to the sopaipillas of New Mexico and the beignets of New Orleans.

Palillas are supposed to puff into downy pillows of pastry. For a long time, mine never did. I consulted with both of my Spanish uncles who were experts like all Spanish men, on anything relating to our culinary history. Uncle Edward told me to throw the dough against the ceiling. If it came down in a couple of seconds, it was ready. My other uncle, who had been closest to my mother, told me sadly, "Only your mother could make good palillis." Now this infuriated me. After all, I was my mother's daughter. So the next morning I set our to prove my heritage.

In my mind's eye, visualizing my mother at the stove making palillas I suddenly remembered her hand moving back and forth as she spooned hot oil over the dough. That was it. When I tried it my palilla puffed miraculously.

Traditionally, on our family rancho palillas were prepared for New Year's Eve or Sunday morning breakfasts. A platter of these little pillows dusted with powdered sugar will disappear in a matter of minutes. They are best served with dark coffee and hot milk. Children need no accompaniment as they don't have time to swallow anything else until the last palilli has disappeared from the platter.

3 cups all-purpose flour
3 teaspoons baking powder
1 teaspoon salt
3 tablespoons shortening (Crisco)
1 cup evaporated milk (Pet) and maybe a little more
2 and 1/2 cups canola oil for frying
Shaker filled with powdered sugar

1. Stir flour, baking powder, and salt together. Using a pastry blender or large fork, work the shortening into the flour mixture until finely blended.

2. Heat the canned milk in a saucepan or microwave until it is warm to the touch. Add enough milk to the flour mixture to make a dough of soft consistency. Add more milk by the tablespoons if the dough seems too dry.

3. Knead dough for 3 minutes and then wrap in plastic wrap. Allow it to rest for 1 hour. Roll out to a rectangle (about 9 x 13 inches), fold in half and roll out again. Fold once more. Cover dough with the plastic wrap and let it rest for 5 minutes so it will be easier to work with.

4. Divide the dough into 4 pieces. Keep all dough covered except the piece you are working with. Roll out 1 of the pieces into a circle. It should be about 1/16 inch thick. Cut into 4-inch triangles. Traditionally, palillas have always been triangular shapes.

5. Heat up the oil in a deep 3-quart saucepan while you are rolling out the first piece of dough. Test the readiness of the oil by dropping in a small piece of dough. When ready the oil should bubble around the dough and turn it golden. Temperature of oil should be 350 to 360 degrees. Fry one palilla at a time by dropping in the dough and spooning hot oil continuously over it. This is the secret to

your success. As you keep spooning oil over the dough, it will keep puffing until it balloons. Fry palilli until golden brown. Remove with a slotted spoon and drain on paper towels. Blot palilla with more paper towels. Continue to fry and roll out rest of the dough. If the oil starts to smoke, turn off the heat for a minute.

6. Use a fine strainer or sugar sprinkler to dust the palillis with powdered sugar. Everyone usually likes to add more sugar to their own palilli.

In the Southwest, they drizzle honey inside the sopaipilla. Also to make sopaipillas, roll out the dough to 1/8-inch thickness rather than 1/16. Sopaipillas are used more as a bread to accompany meals rather than a pastry.

Makes 24 palillas

Cutting out triangles of dough; spooning hot fat over paililla to make it puff; a platter of palillas dusted with powdered sugar.

147

Twirl a molinillo or whisk between your fingers to foam the chocolate.

RANCHO CHOCOLATE

Few people realize that chocolate, preferred in pre-Colombian Mexico, was first a drink and not a dessert. It was readily adopted by the conquering Spaniards and when California and the Southwest were settled by Spanish settlers they drank chocolate instead of coffee in the morning. The soldados de cuera, leather-jacketed soldiers, who protected the missions were given a ration of chocolate to cook over their campfires.

The chocolate beverage taken on the Early California ranchos was thick and custardy much like the chocolate beloved in the cafes of Spain. Just like with Mexican chocolate, it should be whipped into a froth with a whisk or molinillo, the wooden chocolate beater. When made properly, it should definitely leave you with a chocolate mustache.

4 squares semi-sweet grated chocolate
1 cup boiling water
4 cups milk
1 tablespoon cornstarch
3 tablespoons sugar
Pinch of cinnamon
2 teaspoons vanilla
1 egg, beaten

1. Boil the chocolate in the water until melted. Stir constantly.

2. Blend the cornstarch with a little milk and then add to the melted chocolate and rest of milk along with sugar and cinnamon.

3. Slowly drizzle in the egg. Stir the chocolate with a whisk for about the next 10 minutes or until it is thick enough to coat a spoon.

4. Pour into a 2-quart pitcher so you can froth the chocolate. Place a whisk or molinillo between your palms and twirl back and forth to create a foam. Pour into deep cups, spooning froth on tops.

Makes 4 large servings. Accompany with hot, buttered toast, bolillos, or with the tortillas above and you will have a breakfast made in heaven.

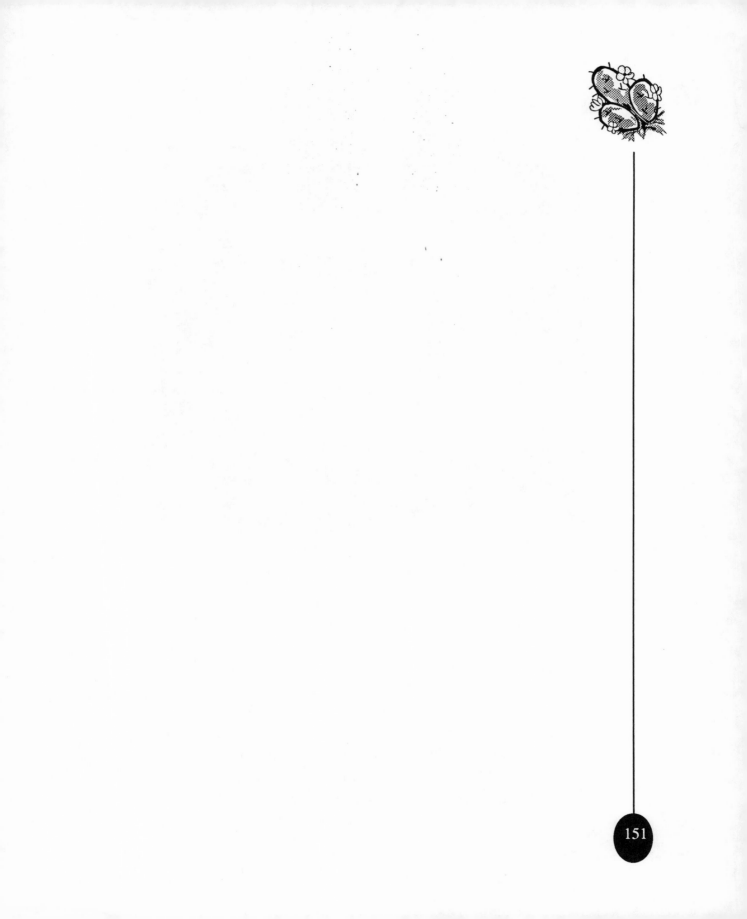

A circa 1940's tablecloth found in a second-hand store became a focal point for the Mexican Breakfast Book because
its colors and homey charm reminded everyone of breakfast
at a favorite aunt's or grandma's table.

CHAPTER IV

REMINISCENCES AND RECOLLECTIONS
OF BREAKFASTS PAST

The breakfasts included within this chapter were the sort of breakfasts that were benchmarks in a young life, my own, but I didn't know it at the time. One usually never does for it is only upon reflection and years that certain experiences realize their true worth.

BREAKFAST AT GRANDPA'S TABLE

One of my first remembered breakfasts was a cup of coffee. My mother had forbidden me to drink coffee (I was only 5) and when she left me for a weekend with my grandparents, her parting words were always "No coffee this time or it will stunt your growth;" and so Grandpa waited until she left and then mixed up our delicious cups of coffee with Pet milk and lots of sugar. The Pet milk and sugar were meant to reverse anything bad.

As Grandpa grew very old the thing about him that struck me the most was his joy in eating long drawn out breakfasts. He walked with his cane tapping the way to St. Joseph's in San Jose every morning for early mass and on his way back he picked up something fresh from the Italian grocery. The crinkling of paper bags and the smell of just baked breads or doughnuts coming through the door meant Grandpa was back from church.

He took his breakfast alone, perhaps because no one else had the endurance for the two hour duration of the event; if I was visiting he allowed me to sit at his table with my forbidden cup of coffee but I was not to chat because he was reading the paper.

He had fruit, heavily sugared oatmeal, a fried egg easy over that was perfect to dip pieces of bread into, and huge cup of coffee that was an important part of the ritual. He cut off small pieces of sharp Cheddar, speared it onto his sharp-pronged fork with the black handle, and lowered it into his coffee. Once he was sure the cheese had been properly warmed in the coffee, he ate it with bread.

While he broke bread and warmed cheese, Grandmama bustled around the kitchen but walked in great circles around his table. If he suspected that he was being slightly rushed, he called for another cup of coffee in which to warm cheese. But while he ate slowly, he appeared to be savoring each bite.

He breakfasted this way until his eighty-seventh year which was his last.

* * * * * * * * *

SUMMER MORNING PEACHES

I was thirteen and had the entire summer to myself. Being a voracious reader, my lamp (or flashlight) was not extinguished until 2 AM necessitating breakfast at an indecent hour-probably 11 AM.

Upon rising I wandered barefoot in my cotton nightgown out across the back lawn to the peach tree where I picked at least four of the largest peaches and carried them back to the kitchen.

After peeling, I sliced the peaches into the same blue mixing bowl that was used for biscuit making and drowned them in ice cold cream. Still in my nightgown I sat down to a feast of peaches for my solitary breakfast.   I can still taste these peaches, warm from the late morning sun, and none have ever tasted as good.

I always felt content afterwards as though the peaches were a divine and secret meal. I never thought to talk about the wonder of warm peaches and cold cream to anyone but when the season came to an end, my mother commented that strangely the peach tree had not produced well that summer as she hadn't found many to pick when she finally got the time.

Sometimes, I have felt a pang of guilt at not really liking some dish in a restaurant that I was expected to like or perhaps it was something elaborate of my own making which elicited disappointment and I think back to the bowl of warm peaches like a longing for the First Apple. And I have a longing for the First Peach.

DINING CAR BREAKFAST

When I traveled back to college in Oregon it was always on the night train leaving from Oakland, California. Sleeping in a berth was an unthinkable luxury and so with all the other college students and mothers traveling with screaming brats (I vowed never to have any), I slept sitting up.

For consolation, Mama packed her delicious fried chicken in a shoe box lined with wax paper and for dessert a tin of cookies. But this was not enough to assuage her guilt at allowing her daughter to plunge into the dark of night without the comfort of a bed. She slipped me a whole $5 to spend for breakfast in the dining car. It was then that an irrevocable pattern for the rest of my life was set forth which was to encompass a philosophy of perfect balance between the ying and the yang; that is any deprivation, no matter how fleeting, should be immediately followed by luxury. I would have gone through all kinds of hell for that breakfast in the dining car.

By 6 AM, my face was washed, my lipstick freshly applied, and my wrinkled blouse straightened as best as possible. I went straight to the dining car to be the first in line. One of the black waiters in his crisp white jacket graciously led me, as though I were a princess, to a table swathed in linen. A pink rose in a silver vase was always budding on the table. There were only three things to order for breakfast but I cannot remember them all. I only and always ordered the French Toast.

It came in all its glory, on a china plate, cut into four triangles, high as a souffle, buttery crisp on the outside and like custard on the inside. You were given a silver server of strawberry jam and English orange marmalade that was too bitter. I went for the strawberry and then set to savoring each bite. It was like nothing I had ever tasted, having grown up on French toast made from sand-wich bread briefly dunked in milk and eggs.

Part of the secret to the Dining Car French Toast was the bread. The cooks cut one-inch thick slices from a home-style bread, like an egg bread. When soaked in cream and eggs, the bread is thick enough to soak up the custard. Every once in awhile someone writes to the Los Angeles Times to ask for the Southern Pacific or the Santa Fe Railroad recipe. Apparently, there are other hungry souls wandering around in search of the real train recipe. The one below is as close as I can come, short of providing the rhythm of the train to help the bread slosh and soak in the cream. The other crucial technique used by the train chefs was to place the French Toast in a hot oven for several minutes after the initial frying. This makes it puff up.

THE REAL DINING CAR FRENCH TOAST

MOST IMPORTANTLY YOU MUST FIND AN HONEST
LOAF OF BREAD, AND IT MUST BE UNSLICED SO
YOU CAN SLICE IT ONE-INCH THICK.
WHOLEWHEAT WILL NOT DO HERE.

10 thick slices of white, egg, or French bread, day-old
5 eggs
2 cups half-and-half
2 teaspoons pure vanilla
2 tablespoons butter
2 tablespoons canola oil
Powdered sugar in a shaker
Strawberry or raspberry jam or even orange marmalade

1. After you have cut thick slices of bread and trimmed off the crusts, slice diagonally in half. Beat eggs with half-and-half and vanilla until light.   Have ready a separate pan to lay out the soaked bread slices.

2. Dip the bread into egg mixture until bread is fairly well soaked and then place it in the separate pan. If bread is oversoaked it will fall apart. Do not keep the bread slices soaking in the egg mixture overnight as some recipes advise. In the morning you will have disintegrated bread.

3. Heat butter and oil in a large skillet over medium heat. When hot, lightly sauté 4 triangles of French toast at a time. Just cook until golden on each side, sautéeing a total of about 2 minutes. As you finish each batch, place on a jelly roll pan and continue sautéeing the rest. Add more butter and oil to frying pan if needed. The trains cooks used a great deal more shortening for frying. Place all the French

toast in preheated hot 375 degree oven for 8 to 10 minutes to puff.

4. Place 4 triangles on each plate and dust with powdered sugar. Serve with jam and marmalade.

SAN FRANCISCO CINNAMON TOAST

Cinnamon toast brings me back to foggy days in San Francisco when I was working as a young teacher in the childcare nurseries in some of the more disadvantaged sections of the city. The school cooks were like the train cooks-they had a few things that they did very well, everyone loved them and expected those things to remain as constant as mother's love and so recipes were made the same week after week and year after year. And no one dared mess with them. Cinnamon toast was one of those things.

In one particular school in the Fillmore District, a cook with a big heart made trays of her special cinnamon toast in the afternoon because she knew many of the children didn't get dinner until very late or maybe didn't get dinner. Her cinnamon toast was thick, sweet, buttery and was one of the certainties in life that came at 3 o'clock every afternoon. By 2:30 everyone was ready.

If there were any leftovers, they were rewarmed for breakfast treats.

8 thick slices of bread
3/4 of a stick of butter
1/2 cup sugar
3 teaspoons cinnamon

1. Trim off crusts from bread and cut slices in half. Brush with a little of the butter and bake in 350 degree oven for 4 minutes.

2. Mix rest of the butter with the sugar and cinnamon. Spread this mixture thickly on each piece of warm bread.

3. Place bread back in oven for 6 to 8 minutes until barely toasted. Do not let it dry out too much. Cinnamon toast is perfect when you bite through a crunchy exterior of sugary cinnamon to a soft interior.

Serves 4 to 6 hungry eaters.

SWISS ROESTI

These potatoes, a giant potato pancake, are so good that they can be eaten with any style breakfast or any time of day with any meal besides breakfast just as they are in Switzerland.

Once my husband and I spent a very low-budget week in Zurich where we rode the trains to different outlying villages every morning as our main entertainment. We ate a lot of roesti potatoes, wonderful breads, and hot chocolate—all keeping us within our budget.

4 large Russet baking potatoes
4 tablespoons sweet butter, melted
Salt and pepper to taste
1/4 cup grated Gruyere, minced ham, or crumbled bacon
(optional)

1. Boil unpeeled potatoes 7 minutes. Drain and cool in the refrigerator for several hours or overnight. Do not use raw potatoes or completely cooked potatoes for roesti or it won't turn out right. Peel the cooled potatoes and shred over a big-holed grater or use the grater on a food processor.

2. Place 2 tablespoons butter into a heavy, nonstick skillet. Place a layer of potatoes about 1-inch thick in skillet, press firmly with spatula. Salt and pepper to taste. Drizzle about a tablespoon of butter over the potatoes, then add another thin layer of potatoes, salt, pepper and a little melted butter. Press down on potatoes with spatula. Before you add the last layer of potatoes you can add some cheese or ham for a filling but it isn't necessary. Add the last layer of potatoes and press.

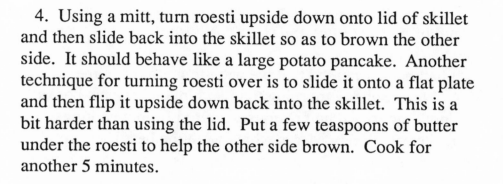

3. Place skillet over medium heat. When you hear butter begin to sizzle place on a lid for 5 minutes. Then remove lid and gently shake skillet to make sure potatoes aren't sticking. This is where a nonstick skillet really helps. Cover and cook for 20 minutes longer or until potatoes are a deep golden brown.

4. Using a mitt, turn roesti upside down onto lid of skillet and then slide back into the skillet so as to brown the other side. It should behave like a large potato pancake. Another technique for turning roesti over is to slide it onto a flat plate and then flip it upside down back into the skillet. This is a bit harder than using the lid. Put a few teaspoons of butter under the roesti to help the other side brown. Cook for another 5 minutes.

Serves 4 to 6 as a side. Cut into wedges to serve.

THE KEY TO SUCCESSFUL ROESTI POTATOES IS TO PRECOOK THE POTATOES FOR 7 MINUTES AND THEN CHILL IN THE REFRIGERATOR FOR SEVERAL HOURS BEFORE YOU NEED THEM.

BILL BRIDGES' TEQUILA BLOODY MARY

Through a good friend I found out that Bill Bridges, a fine photographer whose work has appeared in publications from *Life Magazine* to the *Paris Match*. was leaving his home in Ventura, California and moving back to Texas. He had his entire and impressive cookbook collection up for sale. Besides all this I wanted to meet the man who was also the author of *The Great American Chili Book*.

It had been arranged that we were to go to his home at 10 AM on a Sunday morning to meet him and see his books. Upon our arrival he graciously poured from a waiting pitcher of Bloody Marys which were the best I've ever tasted. A Bloody Mary is just about as good as menudo for a Sunday morning and since we hadn't eaten any breakfast, they were a welcome libation.

My husband, a photographer, was only too happy to chat with Bill about his life's work and thrilled to look at some of his photographs. Meanwhile, he poured us more very tall Bloody Marys. Needless to say, as I tried to peer out at the cookbook titles I was supposed to be looking at, I just wanted a place to lie down.

I did end up buying a couple of cases of old cookbooks from Bill that were real treasures and he even gave me the recipe for the Bloody Marys which were about the most effective sales technique I've ever run into head-on.

5 ounces good tomato juice (like Sacramento)
1 jigger (1/2 ounce) fresh orange juice
Juice of 1 lime
1 tablespoon Lea & Perrins

1 teaspoon Pickapeppa Sauce from Shooter's Hill
1/4 teaspoon Tabasco
1 to 2 drops of Angostora bitters
Freshly ground black pepper or
   1 chile peqin, crushed
Dash of salt
2 jiggers (3 ounces) 90 proof or better tequila

1. Stir or shake all ingredients except tequila. Pour mix over ice in chilled beer glasses. Add the tequila at serving time and stir. I did notice that a real Texan like Bill didn't add anything like cutsey celery sticks for stirrers. Serves 2

2. You can easily double, triple, etc. the above mixture for a large pitcher of Bloody Marys. The amount of tequila can be lessened at the loss of flavor but the gain of motor skills. Try using a fine tequila like Herradura in a smaller amount. Shorter glasses for each serving can also be used.

CHOCOLATE CAKE FOR BREAKFAST

One of the treasures that I found in the boxes of Bill Bridges' cookbooks was a stained little booklet called *Baker's Best Chocolate Recipes* printed in 1932 and written inside the cover in faded ink was a recipe for Larry's Devil's Food Cake. I was compelled to try it because chocolate devil's food was what I always wanted for my childhood birthday cakes. This one is marvelous.

The morning after your birthday or any morning that you have leftover chocolate cake, you should have it for breakfast and it will taste better than at any other time. A good piece of chocolate cake should be eaten without the infringement of other foods.

At breakfast the chocolate can stand on its own.

LARRY'S DEVIL'S FOOD CAKE

4 squares melted bitter chocolate
1/2 cup butter or shortening
1 and 1/2 cups sugar
2 eggs
1 teaspoon vanilla
2 cups sifted cake flour
1 teaspoon baking powder
1/2 teaspoon salt
1 cup sour cream
1 teaspoon baking soda dissolved in 1/3 cup boiling water

1. Melt the chocolate and set aside while you prepare the rest of ingredients. Butter 2 8-inch cake pans and fit with rounds of parchment. Butter also.

2. Beat butter and slowly add sugar. Beat until lightened, about 2 minutes. Add one egg at a time, beating well after each addition. Next add the cooled chocolate and vanilla. Combine well.

3. Sift cake flour with baking powder and salt. Alternate additions of cake flour and the sour cream to the sugar-egg mixture. Begin and end with the flour. Dissolve the soda in the boiling water and then quickly stir the bubbly mixture into the cake batter using a whisk, stirring just till blended.

4. Immediately pour batter into cake pans and bake in preheated 350 degree oven for about 25 minutes or until tester comes out clean.

CHOCOLATE ICING

3 ounces cream cheese, softened
2 tablespoons butter, softened
2 ounces semi-sweet chocolate, melted
2 cups sifted confectioner's sugar
1 to 2 tablespoons hot milk or coffee
1 teaspon vanilla

1. When the melted chocolate is barely warm, beat in the cream cheese and butter. Sift in the confectioner's sugar. Add enough hot milk to make the icing creamy and just thick enough to spread nicely. Spread between layers of cake and over tops and sides. One of my boys' favorite additions are 3 minced Heath bars. Press into the icing along the sides and top.

INDEX

RESOURCES FOR INGREDIENTS

THE CHILE SHOP
109 E. Water St.
Santa Fe, New Mexico 87501
(505)983-6080

Source for wonderful, dried chiles and ground powders especially selected from small farmers. Favorites are Dixon and Chimayo. Carry blue corn products and posole. Have beautiful gifts related to chiles. Christmas chile ornaments and chile books

SANTA FE SCHOOL OF COOKING
116 West San Francisco St.
Santa Fe, New Mexico 87501
(505) 983-7540

A regional cooking school offering classes specializing in the Southwest. Classes always offer a lunch and the school was chosen by the Whole Chile Pepper Magazine as having some of the best food in Santa Fe. Their small retail store offers fabulous ingredients for sale like freshly ground masa harina; fresh green chiles in season (Sept. and Oct.); herbs like epazote; blue corn products; exotic beans; red dried chiles. Also carry equipment needed for Southwestern style cooking.

CHILE PEPPER EMPORIUM
328 San Felipe Rd.
Albuquerque, New Mexico 87104
(505)242-7538

Good selection of dried chiles and Southwestern ingredients. Will send chile care packages.

PEPPERS
4009 N. Brown Ave.
Scottsdale, Arizona 85251
(602)990-8347

Arizona's resource for anything related to chiles and chile gifts.

SANTA CRUZ CHILI AND SPICE CO.
Box 177
Tumacacori, Arizona 85640
(602)398-2372

This small company processes the sweet, hot red chiles harvested only in autumn and makes the Santa Cruz Chili Paste, a great base for chili, enchilada sauce, and barbecue sauces. Also operate small gift store.

"GRIMES IS NOT THE NEXT DOROTHY SAYERS, NOT THE NEXT AGATHA CHRISTIE. SHE IS BETTER THAN BOTH."
—*Atlanta Journal & Constitution*

"ONE OF THE ESTABLISHED MASTERS OF THE GENRE." —*Newsweek*

"READ ANY ONE [OF HER NOVELS] AND YOU'LL WANT TO READ THEM ALL."
—*Chicago Tribune*

Praise for *The Case Has Altered* . . .

"Provocative entertainment." —*Orlando Sentinel*

"Grimes is dazzling in this deftly plotted, 13th Richard Jury mystery. Psychologically complex and muted in tone, with the characters' elliptical relationships reflecting the setting of England's dreamlike fen country, the novel also boasts Grimes's delicious wit. Grimes brings Jury triumphantly back where he belongs."
—*Publishers Weekly*

"A delicious ebb and flow of tension . . . twists and turns . . . beautifully rendered atmosphere."
—*Library Journal*

"Grimes's best book in years." —*Kirkus Reviews*

"A brilliant police procedural, a stately and dignified saraband of a mystery in which diligence, dignity, and deliberation win out over showier, slicker police tactics."
—*Booklist*